The LONGEVITY HOME

Where to Retire to Set Your *(Much Older)* Self Up for Success

RANI GURAM

ISBN: 979-8-218-37833-2

The sample photos of Sonoma in Planning Exercise 3 were photographed by Rani Guram. Cover and interior design by Lorie DeWorken, MindtheMargins.com Cover images courtesy of Adobe Stock

Printed in the United States of America
First Printing Edition April, 2024

Text by Rani Guram

Summary: You can choose to Age-in-Place, to live in the autonomy, comfort, and security of your personal home and surrounded by your familiar and supportive community throughout your senior twilight years. But it won't happen automatically, so plan while you have the energy, patience, mental and physical stamina, and financial resources to find the appropriate home environment to retire in that will best support you to live well, independently longer, in your own home. This book will guide you through developing your personal game plan to find such a place, so that when you choose the place to call home, it will be your forever home, the home that supports your optimum longevity.

Passages marked NIV are New International Version (NIV) Holy Bible, New International Version®, NIV® Copyright ©1973, 1978, 1984, 2011 by Biblica, Inc.® Used by permission. All rights reserved worldwide.

Passages marked KJV: Scripture quotations from King James Version. Public domain in the United States. In the UK, rights in the Authorized Version in the United Kingdom are vested in the Crown. Reproduced by permission of the Crown's patentee, Cambridge University Press.

Names have been changed to protect the privacy of the persons from whom we can learn.

For interactives to use in group studies, see the exercises at the end of chapters 6 -10 of this book.

Websites can change, so please approach any reference to web content with this understanding and caution. Though all links were thoroughly checked at the time of publication, something may have been changed since then.

DEDICATION

This book is dedicated first and most to my Heavenly Father who gives wisdom and understanding that we may live well on this earth and help others to do likewise.

Secondly, I dedicate this book to my beloved grandmother, Maxine Guenther. Her courage, her journey, and persistence to pursue a path to live independently in her own home throughout the last decades of her life (she lived to be 99 years old),even when the journey had its challenges and struggles, is what inspired me to write this book.

I want you, reader, to know that the journey to live independently in your own home, surrounded by the neighborhood and community you feel connected to, as you progressively age through your twilight years, can be a more peaceful and pleasant transition if you plan ahead to choose and create the home environment that will support and set your *Much Older* self up for success.

To help you achieve that peaceful transition, I wrote this book.

⚜

Are you nearing retirement or recently retired? If so, this is the ideal time to plan, to make the right choice for where to retire, and to make it right the first time.

I believe it is crucial that people plan ahead to prepare a home environment that will support them to live well, independently longer, through the last decades of their lives.

It ranks in importance with planning ahead financially for retirement and maintaining your physical fitness to endure the journey of aging.

It's something we *all* need to be ready for.

TABLE OF CONTENTS

❖

PROLOGUE

I, Rani, wrote this book for you because—though none of us want to have the conversations or admit the reality—you and I are getting older. Like me, you may want to stay in the comfort of your own home, in your familiar neighborhood, surrounded by people you have come to know and trust, and keep actively engaged in the community you feel connected to throughout the rest of your life. The most probable way to get this to happen is to plan ahead. This book will show you how to create a game plan for where to retire to set your (much older) self up for success and Age-in-Place gracefully.

The objective of Aging-in-Place is to be able to live independently in your own home, while your aging body transitions to become less independent. Instead of resorting to moving out of your home to go somewhere to receive the help you need to manage your basic living requirements, planning now to Age-in-Place in your own home as you go through the last decades of life will help you prepare for that transition in aging so you can avoid the abrupt changes to your living environment and remain in your own home.

You can have peace knowing that you can continue with what is familiar and comfortable for you and maintain a sense of control over your life and future because of the planning you do now.

Aging-in-place ranks right up there in importance with planning ahead financially for retirement and with maintaining your physical fitness to endure the challenges of aging.

We all need to plan for it!

Ready? Let's make it happen!

❖

CHAPTER 1

Why This is a Must-Read Book for You

"A prudent man sees danger and takes refuge,
but the simple man keeps going and suffers for it."

PROVERBS 22:3, NIV

So you want to stay in your own familiar and comfortable home, surrounded by the community where you feel you belong, until it's time for you to leave this earth?

Here is why you must read this book...

**The thoughtful planning you do now for
where your Much Older You will live out
your senior years will equip you
to live independently longer
and
to live a better quality of life.**

Living well throughout your senior years does not happen automatically. Those who successfully live independently as they progress through the last decades of aging have put in the effort to plan ahead. These people have taken actions to support a good quality of life in anticipation of their journey through their twilight years.

Our society has acknowledged the importance of planning ahead to meet the financial requirements in retirement, when we no longer have a working income.

Our society has also affirmed the importance of maintaining good health to meet physical and mental challenges as we age.

But our society has yet to acknowledge the value of planning for where we will live out the rest of our senior years and how that impacts our quality of life, longevity, and survival.

We find it much easier to ignore that need until we are faced with the challenge. By then it's a rough struggle because we have less energy, less patience, less mental ability, less physical agility, and sometimes less income to make the pivot to move to a living environment that will properly support our needs in our aging progress. Even as you read this you may be thinking you'll never need such a plan. But the reality is we all will face the challenge of trying to remain independent in our own home as we age. Choosing to prepare ahead for a home environment that supports your progression in aging lets it occur as peacefully, as gracefully, and as enjoyably as possible.

What post-retirement living environment will best support the 60-, 70-, 80-, 90-year-old you in experiencing:

- Your lifestyle goals, hobbies, recreation and social activities?
- Your priorities, commitments, relationships, and values?
- Your desire to live independently in your own home, surrounded by a caring and supportive community and neighbors?
- The best quality of life for you, given your limitations, or restrictions?

These are the questions we'll explore in this book.

⚜

We have witnessed the struggle to live independently while aging as we have watched our Much Older relatives and friends who have gone before us. Though this is a struggle we will all face, rarely do we see it done well or learn from the lessons others before us endured. Rarely do we find those who have planned for transitioning through this stage in life peacefully and securely. As we progress in aging, we perhaps assume we can simply keep doing all that needs to be done to manage and maintain our household, our day-to-day living tasks, our health routines, our social relationships, our finances, our hobbies and interests, our commitments and sense of purpose, and our desired lifestyle.

During our later years of aging, the youthful abilities and capabilities we have always relied on to do these things start to dwindle.

We feel surprised when the time comes in our lives when it seems to take more energy, strength, and time to accomplish all that we used to do more effortlessly when we were younger. As the challenges increase to manage and maintain our fundamental living requirements and quality of life, we may start to question whether we can keep managing it all by ourselves. We may even start to feel the fear of being out of control, and that fear can keep us immobilized.

Or we may stubbornly declare we can manage it all by keeping the status quo, when everyone around us realizes we can't.

Pre-planning to live independently well through this later stage in our lives will give us more peace of mind when the time comes. The pre-planning we discuss in this book covers preparing for the right type of three-fold supportive living environment to Age-in-Place, so we can increase our chances to not only live independently but to also continue to live *well* independently.

This book will lead us through the steps of creating our plan for a supportive living environment on three levels:

1. the right town,
2. the right neighborhood, and
3. the right home.

How will all three work together to equip you to live independently longer?

Why is each needed to contribute to your quality of life through the aging process?

We use these three elements of a living environment to Age-in-Place. Most of the world is looking for the answer for how to Age-in-Place, and in this book you will discover it.

> **The U.S. Centers for Disease Control and Prevention defines aging-in-place as "the ability to live in one's own home and community safely, independently, and comfortably, regardless of age, income, or ability level."**

> **"A Report to the Nation on Livable Communities: Creating Environments for Successful Aging" explains that 90 percent of adults over the age of 65 would prefer to stay in their current residence as they age.**

Statistics –and our hearts—both confirm that most of us would like to stay in our own homes throughout our lives. We are familiar with home. Home feels comfortable. We like to be the master of our own fate.

Living at home maintains confidence and self-respect, independence and autonomy.

We want to be around neighbors we have come to know and trust.

We like making our own daily schedules, choosing what we do, what we eat, where we go, and when we do these things. We have earned the privilege of experiencing our home environment the way we want to. But it takes planning to maintain that when we become much older, and our abilities and capabilities start to wane.

Assisted living facilities may mean giving up our independence, some control and decisions, our neighbors and neighborhood, and the comforts and familiarity of home. So let's make plans NOW to try to avoid this in the future if at all possible.

Currently in our society, there is a lack of education and emphasis on the importance of aging-in-place. Unfortunately, most of society has not put much thought into how to live independently success-fully when they reach their 80s and 90s, and the outcome has often been a difficult transition through the last decades of life. Often our elderly are caught off guard on the increasing challenges of man-aging life alone in their later years and some will spend those last years struggling to figure out how to obtain some sense of security, and be in an environment where they feel safe, where they feel they have a sense of control, and are connected with people with whom they are familiar and who truly care about their state of well-being.

In an earlier era, aging parents often moved into the homes of their grown children when their spouse died or when they felt they could not manage their home independently any longer. Multigen-erational families were common, where grandparents often lived with their grown children's family until they breathed their last breath. I see this scenario less and less.

Our American culture has shifted to more adult children leaving their hometowns to build their careers, see the world, grow their own family, and make their own mark on this world. The cultural change of geographically disconnected families started decades ago, but we never came up with a well-laid out plan for how the elderly parents we left behind would be cared for.

Our geographically disconnected families have caused a gap in the provision of assistance that elderly parents had depended on to live out their twilight years...the years that are most critical for one to not feel left alone to manage life while the body and mind become less responsive. How to maintain living independently as we progress through our last decades of life can be a scary challenge for anyone and it will be a challenge we all face. So lets face it together. Keep reading!

We are a culture that values our independence at all ages. Living in our own homes gives us the autonomy to choose how we want to live...we don't easily let go of that sense of independence even to move in with our grown children when we need their help. There is a mental benefit to managing our own domain. When we continue to use our brains to make decisions for ourselves, planning, budgeting, organizing, and all that goes into running a household and living a standard of lifestyle, it keeps our minds mentally exercised.

It is a benefit to society to help our elderly live independently, safely, and successfully.

With the thoughtful planning practices outlined in this book, you will learn to make wise choices for the living environment where you choose to Age-in-Place.

Like any challenge, when you plan ahead for how you will face it, you can have greater peace when that time approaches.

This book will help you create a personal **game plan** to find and establish the home environment that will best support you to Age-In-Place so that the *Much Older You* can age with peace of mind, because of the planning you do NOW.

Use your **game plan** to equip you to make choices to help you live independently longer and successfully as you transition through your twilight years.

Let's Age-in-Place!

❖

CHAPTER 2

We Are in This Together

*"If you want to go fast, go alone,
if you want to go far, go together."*

AFRICAN PROVERB

Being an architect with 30 years of experience designing built environments and specializing in custom residential design, I have become intimately aware of the importance of

- early,
- strategic, and
- intentional

planning in order to create an ideal environment that will fulfill the intended program and usefulness of the space. We will use this planning approach as we walk through the steps of identifying and prioritizing important features to include in your post-retirement Age-in-Place home environment.

I am writing this book two years after both my grandmother and my dad have died. I am building on the lessons I learned as I witnessed them go through their own challenges to live independently while they aged. Their journey and struggles to Age-in-Place prompted me to urge you to be proactive in planning ahead to create a living environment that will support your Much Older self.

How can you choose a living environment that supports you in your quest to Age-in-Place?

How can you experience a good quality of life and peace of mind as you live out your last decades?

Read on!

I witnessed the struggles of my beloved maternal grandmother, who lived to be 99, and of my wheelchair-bound dad, who lived to be 88, as they tried to live independently in their own homes while their bodies and resources slowly diminished and they became more challenged by their minds and emotions. Through the last decades of their lives, they worked hard at trying to live comfortably, safely, and simply. They endeavored to maintain physical and financial stability, stay socially connected, and be healthy. Why? Their lives and their independence depended on it.

These actions come more easily when we are younger. These actions challenge us when we are older. The more you and I can prepare for those days, the more peaceful and enjoyable our twilight years will be. We can go through those years with less fear of the unknown and with more confidence that we will be able to stay in our own homes longer, and live well.

We can live independently in the comfort of and the familiarity of our own home, surrounded by our supportive community and our caring neighborhood. Living this dream will take intentional planning and an open mind to keep learning about how to do things more efficiently, effectively, and strategically. We'll need to discover how to do more with less.

> **"Living this dream will take intentional planning and an open mind to keep learning about how to do things more efficiently, effectively, and strategically."**

I will walk you through creating a personalized plan for bolstering your current home and/or choosing a new living environment to Age-in-Place. Your town, neighborhood, and home make up the three critical components of a supportive and successful Age-in-Place living environment.

In an April 28, 2022 blog entry, titled *"A Key Retirement Reality You Need to Be Ready For,"* Suze Orman, one of America's most recognized experts on personal finance, wrote

"Not only do women, on average, live longer than men, but

quite often women partner up with a man who is a few years older. Add in all the women who are single, and the upshot of all that is that older women are more likely to be living on their own than men.

"According to government data, 43% of women at least 75 years old in 2021 lived alone. Just 24% of men at least 75 years old lived alone.

"The best retirement planning advice for women in a relationship today is to think through what might work best for a much older you who might eventually be living alone."

Think through what might work best for a Much Older You—male or female— who might eventually live alone. This thinking through is the foundational concept of this book, even though it might be difficult to envision. Plan for that time in your future when you are much older and potentially living alone. What would you need for a good quality of life when you are living life alone, independently?

1. What will your home be like?

2. What will your neighborhood be like?

3. What will your community be like?

What will it take to be comfortable and contented? How do you see yourself engaging in these environments? What will bring you the best quality of life?

Orman taught in that same blog post, "If you accept this reality and plan for it, just think of the relief and confidence you will feel knowing that no matter how things evolve, you will be in good shape."

You don't have to do this planning alone.

In fact, engaging with others on a similar journey will help you brainstorm and formalize your plan to Age-in-Place. Two suggestions: First, read through this book with a group of friends, family members, neighbors or co-workers and share your thoughts, experiences, and ideas. Second, visit the on-line community called *Efficiency 4 Life* (Efficiency4Life.com) which was created to support individuals who want to *gain back* their time, resources, and energy *through efficient living*. Efficient living is key to successful aging-in-place. Together we will share strategies, practices and routines, research, products and resources that help us become more efficient, so we can do more with less effort and have more time and resources to use toward things we enjoy, are more meaningful, and that make us thrive.

A designated section on this website focuses on Aging-in-Place. Implementing efficient living strategies and being part of a community to learn from and share your experiences with is key to Aging-in-Place successfully.

Connect with a community who shares your values and common interests. You will learn from others who are searching for how to Age-in-Place successfully, and looking for where to retire to set their *much older* selves up for success. Start asking and start sharing....

What has worked for you?

What wisdom have you to share from experiencing similar challenges?

Together we can solve specific challenges and learn from one another's experiences. Together we can build interests. Together we can reach our intention of living efficiently, independently, and successfully.

Together we can thrive as we age!

❖

CHAPTER 3

An Exemplary Age-in-Place Lifestyle

"Anyone who stops learning is old, whether at twenty
or eighty. Anyone who keeps learning stays young."

HENRY FORD

I had the pleasure of interviewing a 92-year-old Sonoma, CA resident, who is a shining example of Aging-in-Place successfully. She is also a neighbor in my condo complex. For the sake of privacy, in this book I call her Josie.

I knew I wanted to interview Josie for this book because from what I observed, she had figured out how to age well in her home environment. I saw her every morning cycling on her three-wheel bike down the town's bike path. She was typically coming back from her morning ride as I was starting my morning walk. Sometimes I would see her pedaling back home after her trip to the local grocery store. Even in a light drizzling rain she would be out cycling.

When Josie got off her bike to walk to her condo unit, she always appeared to walk with stability and confidence. I take note of people's posture, since practicing good posture exudes vitality and strength. I especially admire those advanced in age who still demonstrate good posture when they stand and walk.

When I see someone who manages aging well, I want to know what he or she did and does to enjoy that state of being. So, I decided to interview Josie about her Age-in-Place home environment.

I asked Josie the questions I am asking the readers of this book to consider when choosing their Age-in-Place location: In your personal perspective, what makes an ideal post-retirement...

1. town,

2. neighborhood, and

3. home to support you to live independently longer and live well?

I asked Josie to share the features she appreciated about her town, neighborhood, and home that are most beneficial to her thriving in her post-retirement life, and what features if any she would add or change to make her living environment more accommodating to living independently as she ages.

1. Regarding the Town, Sonoma, CA

The top features for Josie are transportation services, walkability or bike-ability, a strong sense of community, a variety of cultural events, entertainment venues, and social interaction opportunities to engage in. Josie also wanted access to good medical services, and a country-like setting with good year-round weather. This setting and natural environment accommodates her desire to remain mobile and enjoy being outdoors. The across-town bike path, located within a block of her home, accommodates her outdoor bike riding lifestyle, her main source of transportation, and gives easy access to necessities (groceries, bank, post office, medical services) and to community socialization.

Josie likes Sonoma's small-town feel with its strong sense of community and serene agrarian countryside. Though she has outlived most of her close friends, Josie's grown daughter lives nearby. Josie rides her bike to her daughter's house almost every day and the family makes a point to have a weekly dinner together.

Down the street from where Josie lives is Sonoma's vibrant senior community center called the *Vintage House*. The Vintage House offers gourmet meals once or twice a week in an effort to bring seniors together and avoid isolation. They offer classes in art, language, music, computer use, exercises, social activities, and more. The center provides guest speakers for special topics. These offerings are open for all ages of people in the community; they can participate or volunteer. Sonoma also has an aquatic center with mineral pools where various in-water classes such as yoga, stretching, aerobics, and fitness take place. Each is geared for various ability levels.

One reason Josie chose Sonoma for her post-retirement home was easy pedestrian access to everything she would need for daily living if she could no longer drive. Josie can bike to everything she needs such as the bank, grocery store, post office, hardware store, entertainment venues, shops, theater, restaurants, and the historic plaza for festivities and social connections. Sonoma scores high in walkability and bike-ability to access the necessary businesses for most daily living needs.

> **"Josie can bike to everything she needs such as the bank, grocery store, post office, hardware store, entertainment venues, shops, theater, restaurants, and the historic Plaza for festivities and social connections."**

The ability to get to places you need by your own accord, to obtain the things you need to live, is a significant part of living independently successfully. The walkability of Sonoma not only allows one to be independent of owning and operating an automobile, but it also encourages exercise and social engagement. You can always find people walking down the roads of Sonoma, walking from the quaint residential streets to the historic plaza and to the parks and farmers' market, walking down the tree-lined roads and vineyard pathways, walking down the bike path that crosses the town from

East to West, or walking up the trails leading from the historic cemetery to the tree-topped hills overlooking the town.

Josie appreciates the country-like setting of Sonoma with its tall trees, vineyards, rolling hillsides, and wildlife. She also appreciates living in a famous old town surrounded by extraordinary vineyard landscapes. Numerous historic buildings and properties populate the town. The celebrated historic central plaza is the heart of the town.

The words from the Sonoma Valley Visitors Bureau's newsletter paint this beautiful image: "The Plaza's old adobe storefronts, meandering alleyways, sunlit courtyards and historic landmarks hum with an eclectic mix of restaurants, hotels, tasting rooms, cafes, artisan boutiques, galleries—even a vintage movie house. As for the nature lover, wildflower hikes and stunning hilltop vistas abound within just a short distance. Anchoring it all is the tranquil Plaza itself, whose vast green stretches of lawn and immense tree canopy create a lush setting for picnics, cultural activities and weekly farmers markets.'

Josie prefers this more natural rural environment as compared to living in a city. She believes this setting offers her more to do and see that interest her, compared to what the city could offer her. The moderate weather draws her outdoors year-round. Since her three-wheeled bike is her mode of transportation and access to socialization, the moderate temperature and serene natural environment keep her from isolation—something many seniors find challenging later in life when their mobility becomes limited.

To stay socially engaged and avoid isolation, Josie takes advantage of the abundant variety of offerings at the Vintage House and certain cultural events hosted in the historic town Plaza that pique her interest. Even if she isn't inclined to participate in every option, she still finds it nice to have those opportunities available.

Josie pointed out that Sonoma has changed to become more of a tourist destination with an increasing number of entertainment events, festivities, restaurants, wine tasting venues, and boutique shops now lining the historic plaza. These have replaced the stores that once provided the essential day-to-day necessities. Josie can still easily access the hardware store and grocery store via biking, but it is a bit further ride now. Formerly she could get everything she needed for daily living by going to the town Plaza.

That's something to take into account about the community and neighborhood where you choose to Age-in-Place: they change. Even though you might lose some features you once enjoyed, your town might gain other features that make it more vibrant, sustainable, and accommodating to Aging-in-Place. Research to find out. Talk to your town's Planning and Zoning department, your Senior Center, and real estate professionals to find out what plans are on the board for the future of your town and neighborhood.

"Communities and neighborhoods change. When you lose features you once enjoyed, your town might gain other features that make it more vibrant, sustainable, and accommodating to Aging-in-Place."

Josie appreciates the medical services offered in Sonoma, quality medical services, important for Aging-in-Place. In addition, the local hospital has connections to University of California San Francisco (UCSF) to address specialized medical services that are not offered locally.

Josie pointed out the advantage of transportation services for seniors. These ensure access to goods and services essential for living when one is no longer driving an automobile. Vintage House Senior Center offers local rides to seniors to any location in town. If a senior needs to visit a doctor's office in a nearby town, she can call Vintage House a week ahead to schedule a driver who will pick her up to take her to the doctor's office, wait there until the appointment is over, then transport her back home. What an awesome service!

Sonoma also has public transportation service for all ages to transport passengers to specific bus stops within the county and adjacent counties.

2. Regarding Josie's Neighborhood

Josie, now in her early 90s, purchased the condo she is now living in when she was in her 40s. She bought it with Aging-in-Place in mind, even though that term was not used back then. The top features of her neighborhood are walkability/bike-ability to everything you need, a quiet and safe country-like setting, close enough to family, and easy access to the community senior center and other social engagement opportunities.

The neighborhood surrounding the condo complex is ideal to Age-in-Place. We've already mentioned easy access to everything needed to live on, and easy access to the historic town Plaza where the local festivities, boutique shops, and cafes are located. The neighborhood is within a half mile of the Plaza. A bike path passes through the neighborhood and spans across town.

An asset of the neighborhood location, which was not in place at the time Josie bought the home, is being close enough to Josie's daughter's house that Josie can ride her bike there each morning to start the day with a cup of coffee and a newspaper.

Add to all this the fact that the condo is on a quiet street in a quiet neighborhood with the country-like setting Josie adores. Two buildings down from her condo complex is the vibrant Vintage House Senior Center we mentioned in the previous section. The community supports the Vintage House. Many Sonoma residents volunteer there. Even better, you see seniors volunteering and helping other seniors.

The town of Sonoma is a volunteer-oriented community. Many retirees are involved in more than one weekly volunteer group. Volunteering keeps people engaged in the community and gives each person a sense of purpose and meaning to their time. Who needs a nine-to-five job to give purpose?

Josie loves her neighborhood's open fields, vineyards, and dense trees. Across the street from her condo complex is The Patch, a local garden that grows and sells organic produce for that farm-to-table experience. So, if she is ever wanting a fresh cucumber, pepper, tomato, or head of lettuce for a nice lunch salad, she just walks across the street to purchase it fresh from the garden.

3. Regarding Josie's Home

The top features, besides the location, that Josie appreciates about her home are (1) the ground level (no stairs), (2) the downsized but adequate two-bedroom two-bath size, and (3) having the exterior maintenance and landscaping handled by the HOA. She enjoys a fenced patio area where she can grow flowers or vegetables in planting beds if she chooses.

Before Josie decided to move to Sonoma, she visited friends who had lived there. She recognized Sonoma as the place she wanted to live. So, after graduating college in her 40s (she went to college after raising a family), Josie purchased a single-family home in Sonoma. In her late 40s she also decided to buy the condo unit she lives in now because she had the foresight to know that when she got older, she would not be able to manage taking care of the single-family home by herself. She would need a home that was simplified, accessible, and within walking distance of everything she would need for her daily living requirements. It was her plan to buy and rent out the condo so the rental income would pay off the mortgage by the time she was ready to make the transition to move there.

There are two things Josie wishes she had in this condo unit. First, she would like more sunlight coming into her unit. Her downstairs unit has a north facing patio so there is no direct sunlight coming into her living room and patio. The balcony of the unit above deters the natural light from coming into her space. To fix this Josie is investigating options to add more interior lighting. Lit indoor spaces improve one's mood.

Another feature Josie feels would be helpful is a garage. The condo unit has an assigned carport space with a storage closet. But there are no garages. So, she walks from the carport space where she keeps her three-wheeled bike, down the walkway to her front door, a distance of about 150 feet.

When I first asked Josie if I could interview her for you, my readers, I explained I was writing on the topic of how to choose a post-retirement home for the rest of your life. I wanted to know if she consciously thought about how to choose her home environment location to support her independent living, or if it just happened.

She shared something very interesting with me, something that confirmed why I am writing this book. She shared with me about a job she had early in her career as a property manager for a senior living facility run by a faith-based non-profit organization. While working there she witnessed what residents had to adjust to in their new home environments. She said the units were small and many residents found they had to let go of or put into storage their big furniture and furnishings they had been saving for a lifetime. She learned the importance of downsizing when you move into your post retirement home and only keeping what is useful.

She also said the residents rarely left the building. The housing center offered weekly group transportation opportunities, but the location of the facility did not provide the autonomy Josie enjoys in her current home environment. She likes getting on her bike to pedal around town.

As Josie witnessed the quality of life for the residents in the senior living facility, she decided to plan ahead for how she wanted to Age-in-Place. She took action as early as in her 40s to prepare a place for her Much Older self. Josie took action to face aging in the best manner possible.

When the time came that Josie realized that someday in her near future, she would give up her driver's license, she looked into alternative transportation options. She researched and rode various bus routes in and out of town. She inquired about other transportation options though the Vintage House Senior Center and through health insurance companies. She was determined to keep her independence and mobility.

Josie bought her three-wheel bike and became familiarized and confident riding it before she gave up her driver's license. No one asked Josie to give up her car, but she knew she needed to. At the same time, she wanted to keep the autonomy to get to the places she wanted to go without being dependent on others to drive her there.

Now Josie is facing oncoming macular degeneration. Again, she is preparing for the challenge of aging. She is taking steps to learn about adopting a service dog to help her continue to be independent if her sight fades.

Josie is indeed a planner and a go-getter. She refuses to allow the process of aging to take from her the quality of life she enjoys and deserves. Instead, she sees what is coming and takes action to meet the challenges. In so doing Josie keeps her independence and lives well.

> **"She refuses to allow the process of aging to take from her the quality of life she enjoys and deserves."**

A key thing Josie said is "If you are open minded you will be more willing to learn new things to help you live independently, such as using technology."

Josie uses the internet to

- communicate through email messaging,
- participate in her weekly aerobics Zoom classes the community college offers free to seniors, and
- check up on the stock market.

Josie mentioned that others in her generation, and even younger than her, resist learning how to use technology. This includes operating a personal computer and smart phone and using the internet for email, news, research and Zoom. Some even avoid using hearing aids because they don't want to put in the effort to learn how they work, to adjust to having them in their ears, and experience a new way of hearing. But without the hearing aids we miss conversations and that is irreplaceable. Josie insists if you are willing to get out of your comfort zone to learn about new ways to help you stay and live independently, it is worth the effort.

Thank you, Josie, for being a shining example of successful Aging-in-Place!

PLANNING EXERCISE FOR GROUP DISCUSSION

Reflecting on the insights from Josie's story ask your study group, the following questions:

→ How have you used technology to help you Age-in-Place and improve your quality of life?

→ What do you like about your living environment that helps you Age-in-Place?

→ What are some recommendations of towns conducive to Aging-in-Place?

→ What products and services have you discovered to help you maintain your autonomy?

→ What practices, programs, daily habits, and routines support your Aging-in-Place?

→ How do you live efficiently; what processes or strategies help you?

→ What features about your town fit your priorities for maintaining a good quality of life while Aging-in Place?

❖

CHAPTER 4

The Writing on the Wall and Why You Need to Act on It!

"The king watched the hand as it wrote.
His face turned pale...and his knees were knocking."

DANIEL 5:5-6, NIV

The phrase *writing on the wall* comes from the Bible and means that what is written will certainly happen. For the first reader of *writing on the wall*, King Belshazzar, the news was frightening indeed as it foretold that God had numbered the days of the king's reign and it was coming to an end because the king's actions were found disappointing, and he was about to reap the disastrous consequences for it. But with thoughtful obedience that reader, King Belshazzar, would not have gotten himself into such a mess. Similarly, the *writing on the wall* I am heralding to the readers of this book is that you need to plan *NOW*, to prepare your Much Older You to live independently in your own home throughout the last decades of your life. You do a disservice to yourself if you don't pre-plan for the Much Older You.

**Benjamin Franklin said,
"By failing to prepare, you are preparing to fail."**

This chapter gives a broad overview of how to navigate and plan for that challenging process. As explained earlier, most people want to live out the rest of their lives in their own personal home. Appropriate planning makes it more likely that your outcome will be successful. In the previous chapter I shared with you the personal story of a 92-year-old, Josie, who strategically planned early in life to Age-in-Place and is now doing so successfully.

Successful independence didn't just magically happen for Josie. No, she was intentional in planning for it. In her 40s she worked in management of senior housing for a religious non-profit organization. She applied the lessons from her observations of life at the senior housing facility and decided early in her life to create a plan that would support her to Age-in-Place in her own home. When the time came that Josie could no longer physically manage her 3 bedroom-2 bath single family house independently, she had already secured and prepared another home conducive to Aging-in-Place that she could transition into. Josie was proactive in planning. She observed, she learned from what she observed, and she implemented the lessons learned. I want you, reader, to be proactive too.

During the last decade of my father's and grandmother's lives they found that certain approaches, strategies, people, and the environment that surrounded them positively or negatively influenced their success in independent living. Some actions and people created greater frustration for them. Each lived independently in their own home until a week before they passed. One Aged-in-Place more successfully and peacefully than the other, and both experienced the challenges of aging alone.

During their last five to ten years of life, their physical abilities diminished drastically, which made living independently in their homes even more challenging. Both ended up hiring caregivers to come several hours a day, and then even more hours towards the end of their lives.

The transition from doing life alone to allowing a stranger to come into your home to help you do life isn't an easy one, especially at first. But when you realize you need outside help to keep living in your own home, then you choose to accept that inconvenience of sharing your space and your day with someone. And if you are fortunate, sometimes the people that are your caregivers become as dear as family.

A good social network can help you find a reliable caregiver. My grandmother's first caregiver was a compassionate lady recommended by the pastor of the church my grandmother had attended. The second caregiver, also a compassionate lady, was recommended by the Medicare bathing assistant, and also became very dear to my grandmother and our family. Unfortunately, my dad's choice for his first caregivers turned out to be detrimental, as he did not carefully weigh a person's criminal history, behaviors, and associations.

Luckily, he was blessed to find caring and gracious caregivers in the last years of his life.

Do your research on all the hired services you enlist to help you Age-in-Place safely. Build your social network so when you look for a reputable and caring caregiver, you can ask others for referrals. You may be able to co-hire a full-time caregiver collaboratively with other neighbors who also need assistance. The more planning, creative solutions, and research you do for what your Much Older self will need, the better.

⊰✦⊱

Depending on the type of challenges you face in your aging process, you will find it more or less challenging to live independently successfully. Due to your specific circumstances, it may be in your best interest and safety to seek out assisted living care in your last years.

If you seek an assisted living option, consider progressive care. Some senior living developments offer different housing and level-of-care options on the same property to address progressive care. You may find independent living dwellings, assisted living dwellings, and a nursing home, all within the same senior living community. You may never progress from independent living, but if you do move to assisted living or a nursing home, you will already be familiar with the people in the community, the management, and the processes. Again, be proactive to visit some of these progressive care developments and managed care facilities so you give yourself considerable time to know what to expect and choose the best option for yourself before you need to move there.

Leaving your home to move into a managed care facility can make you feel as if you're a stranger going into unknown territory. Who are these people to whom you are entrusting your wellbeing? Depending on the level of care you receive, you may give up some of your choices about how you spend your days, use your time, and plan your daily routine. Who chooses what and when you will eat, when and how you can socialize and recreate, what you can bring with you, and other familiar things?

Determine to keep your own life purpose no matter where you live. You can decide—and live—your purpose!

Keeping and developing purpose in your life after retirement will be an ongoing process and dedication. Don't allow yourself to lose purpose just because you don't work a 9 to 5 job. That was just one way to live out your purpose. Learn new hobbies, set new personal goals now that you have more time to dedicate to achieving them, work part-time doing something that brings you joy and that you look forward to, engage in community activity groups, or volunteer.

**Purpose keeps you interested in life
and keeps you interesting to others.**

Deciding to Age-in-Place can keep you from the downward spiral of diminishing mobility, reduced mental faculties, and less social engagement. Why? Continuing to live independently in your home keeps you from turning over the management of your life to another. Your obligations, challenges, and responsibilities stay under your careful decisions. You govern your home, finances, lifestyle, and personal routines. This contributes to your mental and physical strength.

⤞✦⤝

While my grandmother was in a skilled nursing facility for only a short time—physically rehabilitating from surgery—I noticed her cognitive processes slowed over that time. The controlled environment of that particular place seemed to hinder her mental aptitude. She even stumbled in her ability to complete sentences. During her time in the skilled nursing facility, she did not have to make decisions or think or do for herself. Others did it for her.

Thankfully her cognitive setback was not permanent. Once she returned home and was back to managing her household, setting her daily routines, and managing her personal affairs, she regained her cognitive faculties. By that time my grandmother had a caring helper who came to her house daily in the morning to assist her with cleaning, cooking, washing, transportation, administrative tasks, and work that needed to be done to keep up her home. Even though my grandmother had help, she was still the manager of her household, and the ability to manage kept her mind sharpened.

My grandmother's physical ability had diminished greatly in her 90s due to arthritis and a low immune system. Even so, her ability to manage, delegate, and instruct remained impressive. She decided she had to be in control of her home and do it well if she was to keep living independently. She lived until she was 99 years old and always had a sharp mind. Her lifestyle and interests kept her mind sharp. Daily she rode her stationary bike, read her Bible and practiced her faith in God, and kept up her rigorous nutritional and health regimen. She liked playing cards with her friends, a number of whom lived on her street. She was always reading the latest articles on alternative medicine and holistic health practices that she loved talking about with anyone willing to listen. She was a living encyclopedia for natural remedies and holistic medical practices. Her curiosity to learn more kept her mind sharp.

> **"Though my grandmother's physical ability had diminished greatly in her 90s, her ability to manage, delegate, and instruct remained impressive. Her lifestyle and interests kept her mind sharp."**

Those who keep an open mind and are lifelong learners will be the most determined to find ways that allow them to continue to Age-in-Place.

My grandmother lived out a strong faith in God. She would listen to Christian preachers on television since she could no longer attend church—her television had an amplifier to assist her not-as-crisp hearing, so you could hear the preaching in every room of the house. Her grandchildren, who experienced this when they came for a visit, will laughingly testify to that. Her faith gave her hope, security, and determination to live. Her confidence in God's provision grew stronger as she grew older because she depended on Him more. The Lord God was her Rock, her Sheild, her Refuge, and her Hope. She would tell of God's faithfulness to anyone willing to listen.

> **"The LORD is my rock, my fortress and my deliverer;**
> **my God is my rock, in whom I take refuge, my shield**
> **and the horn of my salvation, my stronghold."**
> **Psalm 18:2, NIV**

Each of us hopes to live long enough to face the challenge of living independently in our own homes through our 80s and 90s+. When we were middle-aged, we witnessed this challenge with our parents, and we saw their determination to find ways to make it work. Sometimes their efforts and strategies were successful. Sometimes they were not. If your parents have already passed on, you may tend to forget the struggles witnessed and the lessons you learned from their challenges. I emphasize to you that you and I need to understand and carry these lessons forward to help ourselves *prepare* and *plan* for our own twilight years. Learn from what they did well, and what they could have improved, to face your own very similar challenges to live independently and live well as you transition through your later years in life.

"Those who keep an open mind and are lifelong learners will be the most determined to find ways that allow them to continue to Age-in-Place."

It is sobering to think about your twilight years (typically 80s and 90s), but more than likely you will face those years. Your intentional planning during your younger years can help you live out that life stage more successfully, enjoyably, and peacefully. You can continue to grow as a person. Like other significant milestones in life, such as marriage, having children, building a career, and entering retirement, if we don't plan for how to face our twilight years, they will creep up on us and we may not like the results. Short- sighted decisions will hurt us.

"This book will help you come up with your personal Age-in-Place game plan NOW so you will be prepared to live your twilight years gracefully and peacefully."

When you are much older and your body is not as agile, you may face overwhelming decisions about how to keep living independently. Without stamina, agility, and mental acuity, you may settle for less than desirable solutions.

Instead, this book will help you come up with your personal Age-in-Place **game plan** NOW so you will be prepared to live out your twilight years gracefully and peacefully. **You can** Age-in-Place in your own home.

This book will lead you through the decision-making process to choose the best:

- community,   • neighborhood, and   • home

to support your personal journey to Age-in-Place successfully.

To choose the right environments to best support your goal to Age-in-Place requires (1) acknowledging, (2) projecting, and (3) defining what your individual **personal priorities** may be in your twilight years. The personal priorities you will explore in this book will guide you to look into your future, consider your Much Older You, and project what your financial and physical state might be and what the requirements may be to be able to experience your preferences for social engagement and recreational experiences, express and live out your personal definition of purpose, continue your preferred daily living routine activities that bring you joy and comfort, and address your future health requirements.

Defining your priorities will help you identify the most important attributes and features to look for in the

1. town,

2. neighborhood, and

3. home where you choose to Age-in-Place.

This book provides you with thought-provoking surveys to help you discover and chart out your personal plan for creating your

Age-in-Place living environment. These will point you toward what to look for and find.

Again, please check in from time to time to be apart of the development of our on-line community called Efficiency 4 Life at **https://efficiency4life.com/** There you will find support, helpful research, recommendations, strategies, tips, and encouragement to pursue meaningful and efficient lifestyles that will help you to Age-in-Place.

On the website we will explore interesting topics such as recommendations for communities and towns that are strongly supportive of Aging-in-Place, inspiring stories of people living well while living longer, insightful news topics from Blue Zones®, a company that seeks to learn from the world's longest-living cultures to find what they do to live longer well, and learn about the Slow Cities movement that highlights cities that are characterized by a way of life that supports people to live slowly, valuing traditions and traditional ways of doing things...Sonoma, California is one of them!

Look for posts on intriguing stories of alternative post-retirement lifestyles such as living abroad as an expat, becoming a part time resident on a cruise ship, snow-birding between warmer and cooler climates, and seasonal volunteer gigs that provide RV living in some amazingly beautiful public lands.

> "We tend to believe the standard of living we see around us is all what we can expect to achieve.... Let's transform our paradigm of aging from being a challenge to being an opportunity. "

One caution: We tend to believe the standard of living we see around us is all that we can expect to achieve. If you don't have good examples in your life of someone creating a better lifestyle to Age-in-Place, you may not have the motivation to do it for yourself. Perhaps you think the best you can hope for is what you have seen in the lives of your relatives or much older friends and neighbors. Check in with our **https://efficiency4life.com** community to find encouraging stories of aging-in-place lifestyles. You don't have to surrender a good quality of life when you become much older. Be open to changing how you experience life and learn new and efficient ways to do things you need and like to do.

I invite you to share with our on-line community your own nuggets of wisdom. We all can learn from each other. We need each other. Together let's transform our paradigm of aging from being a challenge to being an opportunity.

❖

CHAPTER 5

Timing: When to Make a Plan and When to Execute it

*"If you have a plan for what you want,
you will know what to look for.
If you know what you are looking for, you will find it."*

ANONYMOUS

The things we readily acknowledge as diminishing during the aging process after retirement are:

- our working income,

- our regular social interaction,

- our physical abilities, and

- our mental capacity.

This book is not about how to specifically prepare for these aspects. Many books already written address these. Also, trustworthy advisors can help you plan for your financial needs and medical specialists can help you prepare your body to meet the physical challenges of aging. Each of these areas is essential to living excellently throughout your twilight years, so please do not neglect to plan for them.

This book, however, is about how to **plan for creating the best home environment** to support your Much Older You through the aging process. This book helps you choose the appropriate dwelling, neighborhood and town to support you in living independently longer, with a good quality of life. In the previous chapters we discussed why we must plan to Age-in-Place, now let's talk about **when** *is the* **best time** to plan and execute the plan.

> **"The objective of Aging-in-Place is to avoid unpleasant and abrupt changes in your environment when your body won't do what it used to do. An Age-in-Place home supports this."**

When you are nearing retirement, approximately three to five years out, start planning for the home environment that will help you live independently longer. Once you retire, you no longer need to live close to your job. This broadens your choices of where to call home in the next chapter of your life.

Also, by then, our grown children have typically moved out of the house to embark on their own life journey.

You have a clean slate on which to draw the vision of your post-retirement life. Take a long-term perspective and plan for a home environment that will still suit the Much Older version of you. What if you live well in to your 90s? What do you want your life to look like, and what not to look like?

What if you're already retired?

Start now.

Just don't wait to start planning for your Aging-in-Place home until you are at the point of needing an immediate change in the living environment that you currently have. Planning ahead increases the probability you can continue to operate independently, securely, and successfully in your own home. With considerate plans, you can experience the gradual peaceful transition of Aging-in-Place.

After all, the objective of Aging-in-Place is to live in your own home for as long as possible and avoid unpleasant and abrupt changes in your environment when your body won't do what it used to do. An Age-in-Place home supports the gradual transition of your progressively aging body.

About three to five years before you retire, start the planning process to prepare for Aging-in-Place by creating your program and priority lists as described in subsequent chapters of this book. Start researching and exploring potential locations where you would like to retire. See if these places meet your personal Age-in-Place program and priorities lists. During this time, you have the energy and resources to explore your options so you can make wise decisions, and this process of planning will build your anticipation of embarking on your next phase in life, your retirement years.

> **"Planning ahead increases the probability you can continue to operate independently, securely, and successfully in your own home."**

The reason I recommend you start approximately three to five years prior to retirement—exploring towns you might be interested in moving to— is that it allows you sufficient time to do your research. Also, if you find a place you want to call home but the cost of the home (dwelling) or the cost of living in that town is more than you currently can afford, you can keep working until you build up your retirement savings. If you don't know where to start exploring, search the internet for articles on best places to retire. Look at the article's survey results and compare the categories or characteristics they used for ranking what makes a good retirement place with your personal priority list that you will create from the planning exercises in this book for your ideal 'Age-in-Place' town.

Then visit some of the towns you find that meet your Age-in-Place criteria. Visit one town at least yearly until you decide on the one you want to settle into. You'll need to budget for travel, yet another reason to start this process while you still have income from work.

Next, visit the prospective town in different seasons so you will know how hot, cold, windy, rainy, or snowy it can be. Observe the seasonal population swings and how that makes the town feel. Does the town population swell during its tourist seasons and then transition into a ghost town during the off seasons? Observe the demographics to see if there is an adequate representation of seniors and retirees living there. What other ages are part of the community? What makes seniors thrive in that community environment?

As part of the process, contact a realtor who can tell you more about what that town has to offer retirees and the senior community. Ask the realtor about specific residential neighborhoods in the town where more seniors live and what the attractions are.

Visit the local senior center(s) there to inquire about the activities and services offered. Find out from both the realtor and the senior center where to obtain more information for your research. Your goal is to determine if this town meets the priorities on your list.

When I first moved to Sonoma, I looked for a volunteer opportunity to connect with and give back to the community. When I inquired about helping at the Vintage House Senior Center, the manager recommended I also look into joining the Sonoma Valley Newcomers Club (SVNC) to get plugged into the community. That was one of the best recommendations for someone relocating to a new town. SVNC is part of a nationwide network of clubs called *New Comers* that offers social engagements and groups to connect new residents with others who have shared interests such as biking, hiking, pickle ball, card games, cooking, book clubs, sightseeing, wine tasting, and so on to welcome them into the community and to help them feel included and plugged in...its mission builds a strong sense of community. This social sisterhood has become an important ingredient to living a fulfilling post-retirement lifestyle for many women in Sonoma.

If you are considering relocating abroad to another country for the adventure, a lower cost of living, and more affordable in-home-care services, you may want to do it at an age when you still have the motivation and ambition it will take to become accustomed to a new culture and learn a new language. You will need energy and motivation to develop new friendships and become acquainted with a new community. These social connections can help you navigate how to live in the new culture you chose. Social networks can help you find the best locations and prices for services and housing, how real estate transactions work, how to negotiate agreements for services you will need, and so much more.

Even if you plan to relocate to a new town or a new state within your own country, you still need to plan for the physical and emotional energy it will require to pack up your belongings, relocate and rearrange/organize your belongings into your new home. It takes time to organize and get accustomed to your new space and how you function in it. You may need to do repairs and make adjustments to the space to make it functional to your satisfaction and physical needs. You will need to consider the energy it takes to make new friends, find new doctors, a hair stylist, set up bank and utility accounts, get a new driver's license, sign up for a post office box, find a church or other community gathering place that you affiliate with and feel connected to, and all that goes into relocating. You may have forgotten how much energy goes into developing new friends and developing close enough friendships that you feel comfortable sharing your personal concerns or asking for a helping hand or a listening ear. I recommend if you are going to make a big move, to a new city, state, or country, do it while you are in your 60s or early 70s.

Sometimes people get to a certain age and they don't feel that they can muster up the emotional and physical effort to make the move, so they try to adjust their current environment to meet their Age-in-Place needs. Still, even making home modifications takes a certain level of psychological resiliency, steady nerves and the patience to oversee a home construction project, so don't put off your remodel until you have the immediate need for it...plan ahead and be proactive.

To make your existing home an Age-in-Place friendly home, I recommend you take **action** to start remodeling your home to accommodate Aging-in-Place no later than your late 70s.

Consider that in your later 70s your energy, strength, and patience may be diminishing. Whether you relocate or remodel, consider the extensive energy, stamina, and patience you'll need to make this pivot.

> **"Whether you relocate or remodel,
> consider the extensive energy, stamina, and
> patience you'll need to make this pivot."**

You likely won't want to move multiple times when you are older because of the financial, physical, and emotional toll moving demands. So, choose wisely the first time around. The following chapters will walk you through the process of creating the framework to define your Age-in-Place priorities and develop your personalized strategic plan for choosing the best town, neighborhood, and home for the Much Older You.

❖

CHAPTER 6

Create Your Personal Program for the Much Older You

"Where there is no vision, the people perish."

PROVERBS 29:18 (KJV)

Practicing architecture for over 30 years, I have been trained to visualize things before they become a reality. I visualize how things are to be, and then communicate what I see in my mind's eye. I do this by drawing design plans that detail what the building will look like and how to go about building it. I will use this experience to show you how to create blueprints to build out your vision for your personalized Age-in-Place environment.

With your plan in hand, you will know what to look for. When you know what to look for, you will find it and it will become a reality.

As the architect of a building project, I start the design process by helping clients identify, define, and verbalize their needs and goals for the project. This is called developing the project program. If clients do not know how to communicate what they want in a new home, I recommend they look in magazines and on the internet for images of what their living environment could be like in a future home. Together we choose images that resonate with them and define their project program. From the list of wants they create their list of priorities for their program.

At this stage in design, I help the client to define what they need in a home for their future selves. Then, considering their priorities, I develop the program to meet the parameters of the budget and other constraints. We develop the program of what the home will look like, operate like, and feel like.

"A game plan to live independently longer in your own home, on your own terms, and in your own domain."

"If you know what you are looking for, you will find it."

By completing the planning exercises in future chapters of this book, you will also be able to visualize and define the features for your future Age-in-Place home for your Much Older You. You will define your program of priorities for the ideal (1) town, (2) neighborhood, and (3) home to Age-in-Place. You will articulate your needs and objectives, while considering your restrictions and constraints. By the end of this book, you will have developed a plan to identify the personalized living environment that will best support you living independently longer in your own home, on your own terms, in your own domain. With this game plan, you can go out and find your perfect Age-In-Place home and will be able to communicate your program to others who can assist you. If you know what you are looking for, you will find it.

The aspects of the planning process we cover in this book include:

1. **Timing:** When to start planning and when to execute your plan.

2. **Defining:** Identifying your desires, objectives, restrictions, and limitations that will influence your choice of an Age-in-Place home.

3. **Choosing the town:** Find the city or town that includes the benefits, features and amenities that best meets your personal program requirements to Age-in-Place.

4. **Choosing the neighborhood:** Which one will support your goal to stay connected, keep active, and keep thriving as you Age-in-Place?

5. **Choosing the home** that has the form, function, features, fixtures, and furnishings to support the independence of a Much Older You.

In this chapter's planning exercise, you will create the framework for your Age-in-Place future. To create the framework for your personal program, consider what will be *essential* for a Much Older You to have in your living environment. Take a comprehensive, *long-term perspective* and ask yourself, "What will be important to me when I am in my 60s, 70s, 80s and 90s?"

PLANNING EXERCISE

Write several elements or features you believe will be important to you in your living environment during the decades you will progress through in your post-retirement years (60s-90s). Consider the state or country, the town, the neighborhood, and your personal home (dwelling) that will best support your ideal quality of life as you transition through the last decades of aging. (See examples below to start your thinking.)

→ What would I want and need in my living environment when I am in my 60s:

→ What would I want and need in my living environment when I am in my 70s:

→ What would I want and need in my living environment when I am in my 80s:

→ What would I want and need in my living environment when I am in my 90s:

→ Now go back and write restraints and/or restrictions that may affect you in each of these decades (60s, 70s, 80s, 90s), such as finances, health, relationships, or other challenges.

Examples

In your 60s and 70s your *priority* may be to experience adventures that you had put off during your working years. You may want to live in a town that has outdoor recreational opportunities such as golfing, fishing, hiking, cycling, sailing, etc. Perhaps you want to live near your grown children and be a significant part of your grandchildren's formative years. Maybe you want to live near your friends you enjoy being with on a regular basis. Perhaps you want to become a more integral part of your community and want to engage in volunteer opportunities that align with your values and interests. Perhaps budget is a *priority* and *restriction,* so you need to live in a place that has an affordable cost of living and is tax friendly. Perhaps you want to take up new hobbies and interests and do that while socializing with others, so you want to be in a town that offers access to interesting in-person classes for older adult learners.

For your 80s and 90s you may be thinking more about being close to family members or your grown children to share emotional, social, physical, and perhaps even financial support. Maybe you're a person who is intolerant of long periods of cold weather, and it increases with age as well as the concern of falling on icy surfaces, so you want your home to be in a temperate climate where you can enjoy outdoor activities year-round. Perhaps you desire a walkable community where you can access facilities such as the community center, grocery, bait shop, cafes, church, senior center, and hair salon without needing a car, especially when you are no longer able to drive.

For any age, you might be thinking more about the importance of being near specific medical services you may access more frequently as you age.

Maybe being well connected in a vibrant community with like-minded individuals you relate to who have similar interests, and with whom you enjoy spending time is very important to you. Maybe you want to find your "tribe" you identify with and can easily connect with. This need or desire to feel connected and included is even more significant to your well-being when you are living alone.

Perhaps you are a lifelong learner and enjoy learning new skills such as painting, cabinet making, photography, or playing musical instruments. Having easy access to a variety of interesting adult classes may be a priority to you. Remember and value the intrinsic benefit in developing hobbies, pursuing interests, and engaging in activities that continue to sharpen your mental, emotional, physical, spiritual, and social skills. Continue to feel purpose in your life and significance in your surroundings.

Use this exercise to explore what you envision the Much Older You will need and desire to live successfully.

❖

CHAPTER 7

Refine the Program:
Your Must Haves, Likes, and Limitations

"Learn how to separate the majors and the minors.
A lot of people don't do well simply because
they major in the minor things."

JIM ROHN

This chapter focuses on helping you further refine your program, the framework for your ideal Age-in-Place home. In this chapter you will create your program list of **must haves, likes, and limitations** that will influence what you choose for your Age-in-Place home. Once you create this list, ***prioritize*** the list according to your personal preference or importance. Prioritizing will *separate the majors from the minors.*

It's not a simple task to find an appropriate town to Age-in-Place. What town will accommodate your personal wants as well as your expected limitations, restrictions, and specific needs? What neighborhood will support you living independently well into your 90s? What home will make you feel connected, safe, comforted, maintained, and organized toward a thriving lifestyle to the greatest extent possible through your aging process?

PLANNING EXERCISE

Below, you will create three lists to help you plan:

a. must haves   b. likes   c. limitations

Start with the list of limitations, as this will influence your list of must haves. Once you have written your three lists, *prioritize the items in each list (#1 becomes the most important factor)*. Remember, to create these lists with a long-term perspective, considering what will be significant to your Much Older You as you age through your 70s, 80s, and 90s.

1. **Limitations:** I need to consider these in my Age-in-Place living environment (include the restrictions and restraints you identified in the previous chapter):

#1 _____

   ex. living near dependent relatives

#2 _____

   ex. access to specific medical specialist

#3 _____

   ex. low altitude elevation

#4 _____

   ex. manageable cost of living

#5 _____

   ex. transportation options

2. My **Must Haves** for my Age-in-Place living environment:

#1 _____

   ex. moderate all year weather

#2 _____

   ex. access to healthy and organic groceries

#3 _____

   ex. access to outdoor recreation

#4 _____

   ex. be near grandchildren

#5 _____

   ex. strong sense of community

3. **My Likes** for my Age-in-Place living environment (features that are nice to have, but not a must):

#1 _____

   ex. ethnically diverse community

#2 _____

   ex. variety of cultural events

#3 _____

   ex. alternative health services

#4 _____

    ex. Walkable/Pedestrian oriented community

#5 _____

    ex. co-housing community

The first category to describe is the **limitations** you expect you will face. This may be a sobering task, but helps you reign in your likes and clarify your must haves. Limitations also help you prioritize the features of your 'Age-in-Place' home environment.

The list should consider financial, social, mental, and physical limitations (agility, stamina, energy) that you feel you are likely to face during your twilight years. Plan for those so they won't overwhelm you or derail your plan to Age-in-Place.

To better understand any financial restrictions, estimate your post-retirement monthly income. Investment calculators from financial advisors or internet sites can help you project your post-retirement income based on your investments and savings. Your income affects where you can afford to live and the size or type of home.

In your budget include funds to hire help for cleaning and maintaining your home and consider including the expense for long term care insurance. Be truthful with yourself regarding your financial and physical limitations.

If you have current health issues that cause you to seek regular medical services, you likely won't live in a remote area, even if living in a cabin in the woods in a mountain resort town sounds charming. Be realistic in planning for your Much Older You.

✦

Now let's look at identifying the **must have** items for your program.

Must haves are features you already know the Much Older You will need in your home environment through your twilight years. Your home environment includes your *city, neighborhood, and home*. For example, perhaps due to existing health challenges you know your home must be in a city that offers healthcare services specific to your health needs or is in reasonable proximity to where you live.

Maybe you want to live near your grown children and grandchildren; it is very important to you to be near and engage with family regularly. Perhaps you feel confident that your grown children will still be living in that town when you reach your 80s and 90s.

Maybe your financial situation requires that you live in a state or city that has an affordable cost of living and no state income taxes. It may be important to you to choose a town that offers sufficient low-cost senior services and activities.

Maybe you want to be in a town and neighborhood that offers convenient public mass transit because you expect you won't be driving in your late 80s and 90s and you don't feel comfortable taking privatized transportation service.

Perhaps you thrive on participating in community activities and volunteer organizations. The town you call home needs a strong and vibrant sense of community with diversity.

Maybe you're a person who has a low tolerance for hot weather, or cold, or ice. Consider the limitations these environments might have on your older self. When you are older, you may not have the same limberness and balance you have now. If you live in a region with snow and ice in the winter, you may be homebound during the long winter months. How would you feel about being confined indoors for a season? Does the neighborhood have adequate and well-maintained sidewalks? Are there accessible routes for you to get out and about to where you would like to go?

Do you have certain environmental allergies that would prohibit you from living in certain regions? Right now you may tolerate the negative effect allergies have on your wellbeing. But when you become older your immune system won't likely be as strong. You may have greater setbacks because your body is not as resilient. Allergies can be debilitating. If you plan to endure environmental pressures that are tough on your body now, please generate a plan of how your environment can be set up to support you during seasonal allergies.

You get the idea now: 'must haves' help you be contented and secure. What else might you *need*?

⌁⌁◆⌁⌁

Now write your **likes.**

These items are preferences, but you are open to alternatives. 'Likes' are not as high priority as the 'must haves.' For example, you may like a beachfront community because you like being near water, you enjoy fishing, the sea air keeps your allergies away, and you like the laid back, slower-moving, beach town vibe.

Or you may like living in a 50+ planned community because it may be nice to be around neighbors who are living on a similar post-retirement schedule and enjoy similar senior activities. Maybe the neighborhood is quieter and more subdued.

Perhaps it would be nice to have a newer, energy-efficient, low-maintenance home because you don't want to deal with significant repairs or laborious and costly maintenance that comes with older homes. Keeping home operations and maintenance costs minimal will be kind to your post-retirement budget.

Perhaps it would be nice to live in a co-housing community because you are looking for that feeling of connectedness with your neighbors and a sense of belonging to a tribe.

Maybe you want your home to have easy access to outdoor walking paths or biking paths, because these are activities you engage in daily and these help you care for your health.

Perhaps you want your neighborhood to be within walking distance of a pedestrian-oriented town center so you can easily access restaurants and shops and keep yourself socially engaged with your community.

What else might you *like*?

"Plan for limitations so they won't derail your plan to Age-in-Place."

In the following chapters, you will use your lists to start identifying characteristics for the type of (1) city, (2) neighborhood, and (3) home that best suits your personal program for Aging-in-Place. This becomes your game plan with which you choose where to retire to set your (*much older)* self up for success.

❖

CHAPTER 8

Choose the Right Town to Age-in-Place

"A town's vibe is its culture and its soul. Its soul is more important than its outer beauty. If it's vibe resonates with your soul, you have found your Home town."

ANONYMOUS

When choosing an Age-In-Place living environment that will be supportive and satisfying to you throughout your aging process, it is imperative to take a comprehensive perspective and approach. The degree of satisfaction you have in your home environment is affected by the characteristics of not only your personal dwelling, but of your city/town and neighborhood as well. In this chapter we will analyze what characteristics and features to consider in choosing a city/town that will support Aging-in-Place.

An October 2021, *US News* article, compared 150 of the largest metropolitan areas in the country for potential places to retire. The study included data on housing affordability, happiness, desirability, retiree taxes, the job market and access to quality health care, and was weighted based on a *US News* online survey of people aged

45 and older about their retirement preferences. When looking at what was used to rate happiness and desirability, the survey used characteristics such as plentiful and varied entertainment opportunities like museums and sporting arenas, as well as outdoor recreation activities, and a significant senior population to identify and associate with.

What makes an ideal town for *you* to live in during your post-retirement years is based on *your own personal preferences* of what you enjoy and what makes you happy, what you need, and your personal priorities in life.

Now it's time to create your own personal list of characteristics and features of the ideal town to live in that will best support you to Age-in-Place.

Use the space below to write down your initial thoughts about features and characteristics you believe would make an ideal town to retire to and Age-in-Place, then continue to read the rest of the chapter on recommendations of what to consider when making your choice.

In planning for Aging-In-Place, remember to take a long-term perspective of what the Much Older You would find important in your living environment. Consider that your Much Older You may be living *alone* in your 80s and 90s. Sometimes we make decisions based on the perspective of our current situation, but I am asking you to plan ahead for a time when your circumstances and state of being will be different.

PLANNING EXERCISE

1. First, describe what you **appreciate** in your **current town** that you believe will support you in Aging-in-Place. You can write adjectives, phrases, or draw a picture to describe what you value in your current hometown.

   a. _____

   b. _____

   c. _____

   d. _____

2. Then, list the description of the features **you wish** your **current town** had to be more supportive of Aging-in-Place. Start adding words or images that will tell the story of your ideal vision. You might want to create a collage of your vision. Think about Josie's story, and how she was able to identify and prioritize what would be important in a town that would help her age-in-place.

   a. _____

b. _____

c. _____

d. _____

3. In the vision you are creating of your ideal town to Age-in-Place, include **activities** you hope to be involved in during your 60s, 70s, 80s and 90s. See below for examples.

a. _____

b. _____

c. _____

d. _____

Examples

Maybe you would like to be in a town that offers access to yoga and Pilates, venues that offer your genre of live music, adult community classes for dancing, tai chi and art, cultural events at a vibrant community center, opportunities for fishing and golfing, organized team sports for seniors such as pickle ball or bocce ball. Maybe you would like to be in a city with a vibrant downtown with a centralized gathering area where you would enjoy meeting weekly with friends for coffee or lunch, gathering at the local pottery or craft shop, or taking a stroll around the park. What activities can you see yourself enjoying well into your 80s and 90s? Give careful consideration to those, because it is important that you live near these for ease of access and to keep you active and socially engaged.

The description you create for your ideal post-retirement hometown will help you **define** and then **prioritize** what is important to you in your future Age-in-Place living environment.

4. Next in your planning exercise, take from your descriptions of an ideal town which you listed above and considering your list of likes, must haves, and restrictions you described in the previous chapter, make a **prioritization list** for what is **most important** to you in your post-retirement town. See below for examples.

- Your **top priorities** for a town to Age-in-Place are:

a. _____

b. _____

c. _____

d. _____

Examples

Some priorities might be to live close to family members, near interesting entertainment and educational opportunities, access to good medical services or the specific medical services you know you will need, lower local and state taxes on your retirement income and home and an affordable cost of living, a pedestrian-oriented town that is easily accessible by walking, temperate weather year round, easy access to a variety of outdoor recreation activities appropriate for seniors, and to have a town with a strong sense of community where you feel you have found your tribe.

You decide what is important to you; this is your personal plan for your ideal town to Age-in-Place.

✦

I selected the following characteristics as priorities on my list for the ideal post retirement town:

a. supportive and tight-knit community with a quaint small town feel that is easy to be connected in and meaningfully a part of,

b. a vibrant town center that is easily accessible with a variety of interesting shops, cafes, cultural events, and community activities to engage in,

c. a town where the senior population is actively engaged in the community, socially and physically, and where there are a variety of interesting volunteer opportunities to contribute back to the community,

d. easy daily access to outdoor recreation areas to keep me motivated to stay fit. and

e. access to good medical services including regenerative and nontraditional medical services,

f. access to healthy and locally-grown food choices and a wide variety of organic produce,

g. access to interesting cultural, educational, and creative learning opportunities that stimulate and support the health of mind and body,

h. a town I feel safe in,

i. a sustainable town that has all of the amenities, services, and goods that I need to live.

When you start exploring to look for your post-retirement town to Age-in-Place, refer back to this **priority list** you are creating now. It will help steer you in the direction of finding this special town.

Considerations

Below are some **considerations** to think about as you compose your preference list for your ideal post-retirement town:

You may want to live in the city that your grown kids live in because you want to be near them and actively engaged in your grandchildren's lives. Perhaps your grown children have asked you to live close to them so that they can support you as you age.

Consider also that your grown kids might receive a job transfer or move for another reason to a new state or country during the years you are physically unable to make that life pivot with them.

Consider the impacts of cost of living on your quality of life. Will your expected monthly post-retirement income meet the ever-increasing costs of living including basic housing needs, utilities, food, transportation, clothing, property taxes, and the cost for personal help when you no longer can manage to operate and maintain your home yourself? Do you need to live in a town where the dollar will go farther?

Living in a quaint touristy town may offer excitement, but the lack of access to a variety of specialized medical services or public transportation options and senior services may outweigh the advantages. You may not be able to easily drive to another town to obtain these services if you are in your late 80s and 90s. A taxi ride or alternative transportation might not be available or financially feasible. Living in smaller resort towns typically equates to higher prices for housing, property taxes, groceries, products, and services because of limited business competition and higher expense to bring products and services to remote areas. This could also detract from your overall quality of life. You don't want to be continually worrying that your money will not outlast you. You want to have enough money to enjoy the things you appreciate about your town that are not free, such partaking in the boutique restaurants and coffee shops, social events, participating in interesting community classes, and enjoying musical entertainment and festivals, etc.

Whatever type of town you choose, consider the availability of public transportation options. Smaller towns, though quaint, might not provide the public transportation you need, or even privatized transportation like Uber or Lyft services.

Consider that you will most likely be visiting the doctor more frequently when you get older and will have more difficulty getting in and out of the car and might need transportation assistance. Does your ideal town offer senior services such as transportation assistance?

When I was researching privatized transportation options, like Uber or Lyft, for my wheelchair-bound father to schedule a ride to and from the doctor's office, there was mention that Uber accessible vans were on the horizon, but not yet available. If wheelchair accessible vans were not available in a big metropolitan area like he lived in, they certainly wouldn't be available in smaller, less populated towns.

There were senior community services that offered vanpool rides, but in that scenario my dad would not be the only rider, and he would have to wait for several stops before he reached the doctor's office and go through a similar multi-stop process before he made it back home.

Due to my dad's specific health limitations, he couldn't manage to wait that long. Each time my dad wanted to leave the house he had to hire a private driver to drive his personal car and to assemble and disassemble his scooter, which was stored in the trunk.

I share this story with you so you will take a long-term perspective on your planning process. Having reliable and readily available transportation when you are in your twilight years is important to feel secure and be independent. It might even be important to your survival under some circumstances.

If your town doesn't have public transportation services, plan to have enough savings to pay for a personal driver.

If you need to go to a medical specialist in another town and you are unable to drive yourself, consider how you would get there.

You may not feel comfortable asking a neighbor to drive you to another town and wait there until your appointment is completed. This is one example of why it's important to consider being in a town where you feel closely connected and able to build strong friendships so that you can reach out to them when in need of a helping hand.

Does your ideal town have sufficient senior services available? Does it have a thriving community center that keeps seniors actively engaged in the community? A community that has planned gathering spaces that foster intentional community interaction with activities seniors would enjoy, such as bocce ball courts or a central town plaza, will open opportunities to help you create important connections and form new relationships.

Does your town have senior services, free or for hire, which will support your daily living needs, such as cooking, cleaning, and personal daily living assistance? If you have long term care insurance, are there service providers in your town? Long term care insurance will be very helpful in your desire to live independently longer. It's important to do your research on what benefits the different types of insurance will cover. If you get to a state of physical being where you cannot manage your household and your personal day-to-day living requirements, but you want to stay in your home, will your insurance benefits cover the activities you cannot do for yourself?

Do you want to live in a walkable town, where you can still access the things you need day to day without having to drive, especially when you are at the state where you no longer can drive yourself? Historic towns, established before the automobile, were laid out for pedestrian accessibility. This fostered community interaction. In historic European countries, you often find a town center with a central plaza for community gatherings. I have experienced this design concept in historic Spanish and Italian towns. The plaza was the space where the town congregated for regular socializing, celebrations, and relaying important town-wide communications. Present-day land planners acknowledge this design is still relevant today as the cornerstone to building a strong sense of community. Does your ideal town have a central congregating area, an Olde Towne square, that is accessible by walking or biking from your home? This and other community fostering features can help you stay connected and engaged in your town as you Age-in-Place and keep you independent and mobile beyond the days when you can no longer drive.

Look for features in towns that help you find and connect to your "tribe," those with whom you closely connect and who "get" you. Such connections help you live longer independently. Like the African Proverb says, *"If you want to go fast, go alone, if you want to go far, go together."*

What activities do you want your ideal town to offer? If you are a person who enjoys outdoor recreation, does your town offer those opportunities and is the climate conducive to it?

I am a person who enjoys outdoor recreation...in fact, I find that I am happiest when I am outdoors in nature, whether with others or alone. Having access to a hiking trail and cycling near my home is important to me as I age. I see myself engaging in these activities as long as I can keep mobile, and they will help me keep mobile.

I acknowledge that the incline and distance I go will change as I age, but I will find a way and adapt to keep moving. That is the key.

I once lived in a ski resort town and enjoyed the easy access to downhill and cross-country skiing. Historic mining towns of Colorado that turned into ski towns attract many outdoor sports enthusiasts. But some historic towns don't have adequate sidewalks or accessible routes. I did not see many older senior residents or those with physical disabilities as full-time residents in the ski towns I lived in, especially not during the winter months.

Being at higher altitudes, with less oxygen, and enduring long winters with icy walkways and roads makes ski towns a challenge to much older residents. Taking the long term perspective to plan for my much older self in my 80s and 90s, I've altered my desire to live in a ski town to living in a quaint, small, picturesque, semi-rural town that offers beautiful and safe, somewhat level, walking and biking trails, community sports like bocce ball and pickle ball, amenities like golf courses and a community aquatic center, and interesting community events that stimulate the mind and build togetherness. I want all this in a location that has relatively temperate all year weather, surrounded by a beautiful natural environment, so I can keep active outdoors year-round.

My current town fits this description. I currently live less than a block away from a biking/walking trail that runs East to West across my town. Starting at 7 AM and into the evening, I see people of all ages and abilities walking, running, and cycling on this paved trail. The quaint town I live in is a walker's paradise. You don't need a car to access the necessities of grocery shopping, post office, banks, churches, and schools. Even the town plaza, local parks, Pilates and yoga studios, boutique restaurants, world-renowned wineries, movie theater, community center, churches and synagogues, and our happening senior center are within walking distance for many residents, and definitely bikeable to most all.

When I first moved to this town, I would ask people who have retired here what they enjoyed doing for fun around town now that they have more personal time. So many said they volunteered and they walked. I was a little taken back with the response about walking. But the longer I lived here I saw that walking around our quaint town and neighborhoods, through the historic cemetery and trails, and along the vineyard paths, was not only a way of enjoying our serene landscape while getting some physical exercise, but it was also used as a mode for socializing. Walking is one activity that keeps the retired community here thriving both socially and physically. People in this historic town don't stop being active when they retire. Instead, they redirect their energy and time to give back to the community and become more connected to the community through volunteer work and engaging in community events and activities.

> "Walking through the historic cemetery and along the vineyard paths was not only a way of enjoying our serene landscape while getting some physical exercise, but it was also used as a mode for socializing. Walking keeps the retired community thriving both socially and physically."

Alternatives to Consider for your New Hometown

Most people consider retiring in an area with which they are familiar. Often people retire in the town where they have established a career and raised their family because they have become connected to their community through career and family activities. From this they have developed close supportive friendships over the years. Others return to the town of their childhood for similar reasons. But others might decide to explore and adventure into other cities or states, leaving behind familiarity. Some even decide to live in a new culture or overseas.

Oversees living has great benefits to consider. Not only does it offer the excitement and adventure of living abroad as a world citizen, but the cost of living is often more affordable. The cost for goods and services and the paid help you most likely will need when you can no longer physically manage your home alone may be more affordable and easier to obtain.

Because certain cultures do not rely heavily on dependent care services and facilities to provide care to their elderly as the United States has become more accustomed to, they tend to have in-home help more affordable and available.

There may be drawbacks with living overseas, depending on the location, such as lack of high-quality medical services and specialized health care services that you are used to receiving in the United States. Also, you might not fully overcome the language barrier and that may make you feel somewhat isolated and not truly understood. If you let it, it can hinder you from developing deeper relationships.

⚜

The sister of a good friend of mine had adopted a baby girl from Guatemala. They initially lived in a ski resort town in Colorado. However, the young girl never felt like she quite fit in as it was a predominantly Anglo population. So the mother, a single mother, decided she and her adopted daughter would move to Mexico and start a new life there. They decided to settle in a historic resort town in Central Mexico. The town is a World heritage site with a large expat population, an artist community, and has a thriving central historic plaza that the town congregates in.

The mother and daughter have adapted quite well and have immersed themselves in their new community, language, and culture. The mother draws enough income from the rental properties she purchased in the States that she can devote full time to the care of her daughter. The cost of living is so affordable there that she lives a high quality of life at relatively minimal cost. This woman had previously had to work several jobs to keep up with the cost of living in the Colorado resort town.

As you could imagine, this was a bold move for this single mother. She didn't know anyone in the town, nor the country, that she had chosen to make her new home. But she had a goal, and a "why". She wanted to provide a home environment that her adopted daughter would feel connected to and thrive in. I asked her how she was able to make overseas living work for her and her daughter...there must be some lessons learned, as it is not something you hear about every day. She explained that when the idea came to her, she set out to research as much as possible the concept of expat living. There are many books available written by people who have adopted the expat lifestyle, and they share how they made it work for them. You just have to have an open mind, and the desire to make a change, then do as much research and preparation as possible to equip you for the adventure.

Sometimes making a move away from what you are familiar with can be scary, but the quality of life you can receive in return for your bravery is worth it. Sometimes we just need to see beyond what we are familiar with and open our hearts and minds to consider other options that can help us achieve our goal to live independently longer and live well.

As mentioned earlier, one thing to consider about living overseas is that if you move to a region that doesn't have the level of medical care you know you will need, then create a plan of how you will obtain it. If your plan is to fly back to the United States when you need to receive specialized medical services from a specialty hospital, consider that when you are older in your 80s and 90s, you may not be able to travel so easily. Create a plan that is feasible for the Much Older You.

If you are interested in what the expatriate lifestyle could be like, then research it. With the increasing amount of information shared on the internet, the World Wide Web, it is becoming easier and easier to live abroad and learn from others' experiences on how to do it. I recommend you read an article or two on expat lifestyle to get your imagination juices flowing on the possibilities of this type of home environment to Age-in-Place. Maybe you will discover a location, community, or lifestyle you never considered before, and it may perfectly fit your list of Age-in-Place priorities.

Now, for another type of post-retirement community you may not have thought about: ever consider living the yacht lifestyle?

A friend's parents had decided to downsize after they retired. They sold the family home and moved into a retirement community. It didn't take them long before they realized they wanted a different lifestyle than what the planned retirement community offered. So, they sold their home in the retirement development and bought a yacht. They rented a live-aboard slip where they could park the boat permanently. They stayed regularly at one marina as their home base, and then visited other marinas and towns to explore. They developed community and neighborly ties with other residents docking in the marina.

Now realistically, I don't consider the yacht life a long-term post-retirement lifestyle option, because it takes a level of physical balance and strength to manage, maintain, and live aboard your own boat and you need to be agile to weather the storms. And you may not have your same sturdy sea legs in your late 80s and 90s. It's also costly to maintain a boat. I recall a sailor friend saying that BOAT stands for Bring Out Another Thousand.

Another option to retire on the water, that is more like condo living, is to live part of the year on a cruise liner. Search the internet for articles on retirees who live on cruise ships; you will be surprised how popular the concept is. I mention these alternative lifestyles to entice you to get your mind out of the box of what we traditionally think of as a retirement living environment.

What might be **alternatives** for your post-retirement hometown or community?

In the space below, make a list of some alternative living environments you would like to research and list the features and benefits you value in these environments.

1. _____

2. _____

3. _____

4. _____

❖

CHAPTER 9

Choose the Right Neighborhood to Age-in-Place

"Neighborhood satisfaction plays a role in community satisfaction, whereas housing satisfaction plays a role in home satisfaction. Both community satisfaction and home satisfaction, in turn, play a role in life satisfaction."

M. JOSEPH SIRGY AND TERRI CORNWELL, SOCIAL INDICATORS RESEARCH, JULY,2002

Now that you have chosen the city/town where you want to live, let's discuss what you should look for in the neighborhood where you will retire. I refer to the area within a 15- to 20-minute walking distance from your home as being your neighborhood.

What will be important to you to have within proximity to your home during your aging process, through your 60s, 70s, 80s, and 90s?

Let's start planning to identify your ideal neighborhood by doing a similar planning exercise as previously completed for envisioning your ideal city/town to Age-in-Place. Use the blank section at the end of the chapter titled **"Neighborhood Vision Board"** to draw images and/or write words that express the characteristics, features, amenities and values you appreciate about your current neighborhood, then add to the vision board other things you wish it had and would like to experience in your ideal post-retirement neighborhood to support Aging-in-Place.

Perhaps you envision being in a quiet older neighborhood with tree-lined streets having cottage homes with shallow front yards and cheery front porches, where you know your neighbors who regularly walk by your home and stop to chat with you. Draw on your vision board some features you would like to experience, such as a neighborhood park with designated walking and bike paths, a local corner store/coffee shop as your "3rd place" or a historic town square lined with cafés, fun shops and a gathering space for live music.

A "3rd place" is a land planning term for a local "hang out" like a coffee shop or local pub that is easily accessible from your home and provides a welcoming, comfortable, familiar environment that invites you to connect with your neighborhood friends or enjoy personal time like reading a good book without feeling isolated or alone. The 3rd place is the local 'go to' place to know what is going on in town and to reconnect with friends and neighbors.

Perhaps you want easy access to the community park's yoga or tai chi classes to help keep you fit and a reasonable walking distance to the local community center to keep you socially engaged.

Maybe your interest is being involved in a community garden where neighbors congregate and enjoy sharing the bounty of the land that they tend together.

Maybe you envision being in a lakefront cottage community with your fishing boat at the dock, kicking back at the crab shack or sitting in the local pub with familiar and friendly faces...just start dreaming. Remember to consider what your 'Much Older You' would be able to enjoy. Plan for your Age-in-Place transition, from your 60s to your 90s.

One thing to remember is that *what* you surround yourself with in your neighborhood will most likely be the activities you gravitate toward and that become part of your daily lifestyle routine.

We tend to do the things that are easily accessible. If you have to drive more than 30 minutes to get to a park for a walk, then more than likely park visits won't be in your daily or even weekly routine. If you live out in the country and your friends have to drive 30 minutes from town to visit you, you most likely won't have as many visitors as often as you would like.

✥

A friend of mine told me about her grandmother who lived in a house in a well-to-do hillside neighborhood in beautiful Marin County, California. Her grandmother had once raised a family there and never moved away after she became an "empty nester." She continued to live in the house, though it was more than what she used, needed, or could manage.

Though she lived alone she depended on her son's family to visit weekly to help her manage her household and provide her essential living requirements. She refused to learn how to use the computer and thus missed out on the conveniences of utilizing internet services such as on-line ordering of groceries and other household goods that could have helped her be more independent. She was dependent on her son's family to provide her day-to-day living necessities so she could continue to live in her home.

Because she lived on a hill, she couldn't manage to walk down and back up the street to socialize, nor exercise, due to the incline. So, she stayed indoors, and her physical ability diminished increasingly.

Her lifestyle and quality of life reflected the decisions of someone who did not consider a long-term perspective for Aging-in-Place independently. She had believed that having money and family was all she needed to be able to live in her home for her lifetime. But that was short- sighted, because her son and his family started seriously thinking of relocating out of state to someplace less populated with a lower cost of living so that they could prepare for their own post-retirement lifestyle and how they would Age-in-Place.

⚜

Once you create your vision of an ideal neighborhood in the "Neighborhood Vision Board" exercise, create a **list** ranking your **priorities** under the planning exercise section titled "Neighborhood Priorities."

Next to each priority put the decade that you would most appreciate that aspect of the neighborhood. For example, having a local grocery and a senior community center within walking distance might be important during your late 80s and 90s when you might not be able to drive. Being in a lakefront home community with access to a boat slip might be more desirable to you in your 60s, 70s, and 80s, but taking care of a boat might be too demanding in your 90s. Having a walking and or bike path within walking distance and pedestrian access to entertainment and a 3rd place might be important throughout your 60s, 70s, 80s, and 90s. You get the idea.

Considerations

The following are some considerations in creating your list of priorities:

Do you prefer living in a neighborhood that has similar demographics to your age group, as it may make it easier to develop new relationships, since it is probable that there would be members of the community with similar interests, lifestyles, schedules, and personal priorities and preferences that you feel you will relate to?

Collaborating with others in your neighborhood who are also trying to Age-in-Place can present creative opportunities and solutions for the ways you secure and obtain services to help in managing your households and personal needs. For example, you and a couple of neighbors could together contract weekly home/yard maintenance services (cleaning, washing, landscaping, etc.) and personal care services (administrative tasks, private transportation, cooking, etc.) so that you can guarantee the providers a regular number of hours per week and thus negotiate a more reasonable price for these services.

Or perhaps you prefer to live in a neighborhood that has a diverse representation of age groups because you appreciate being exposed to a variety of interesting social and cultural activities, conversations, and life perspectives. Intergenerational communities can provide the opportunity to create neighborhood programs that build healthy collaborative and symbiotic relationships between the generational age groups. Young or middle-aged adults could help elderly neighbors with tasks requiring a level of physical ability that an older resident may no longer possess, such as cleaning out roof gutters or mowing a lawn, and in exchange for their help, the older neighbor might offer to watch the young family's kids after school until their parents arrive home from work. Each generation has something to contribute to develop a cohesive and supportive community atmosphere.

⌖

Try to envision what types of things and places you would like to have within a short drive or walking distance from your home when you are in your 80s and 90s.

Is living near, even within walking distance, to a vibrant and engaging senior center or community center offering senior oriented activities to engage in regularly, such as art, exercise, and weekly lunches an attribute you highly value?

Do you predict the need to be near reliable public transportation to have access to the necessary facilities and services you will rely on and frequent regularly? Do you want to be within walking distance of the local town square with shops, bakery, cafes, or near a park? Are you someone who is very involved in your church or other local philanthropic organization and would prefer to live close to the location where they gather?

Keeping actively engaged in meaningful social connections and physical fitness activities to stimulate your mental, emotional, and physical state are important aspects for Aging-in-Place successfully.

What activities do you envision your 'Much Older You' will be engaged in and where and how might you spend your time in a typical day and or week?

Do you like gardening without the responsibility of all the effort that goes into preparing and maintaining a garden? Then perhaps you want to live near a community garden, not just to get your hands in the soil, but also to enjoy socializing with like-minded stewards of the land.

Do you see yourself playing bocce ball, pickle ball, or swimming with a masters group on a regular basis? Would you benefit from having these amenities and facilities within walking distance from your home?

"What you surround yourself with in your neighborhood will most likely be the activities you gravitate towards and become part of your daily lifestyle routine."

Does your ideal neighborhood have a "3rd place" you would enjoy?

In the 1990s a new land planning concept called "New Urbanism" blossomed and it focused on creating walkable towns and pedestrian-oriented developments that promoted positive and intentional community interaction.

There was a move to create density in urban environments that encouraged smaller homes with shallower yards and creating the "front porch" or "sesame street" neighborhood environment that fosters strong community connectivity and walkability. This concept not only helped build and strengthen the sense of community, but it also helped reduce urban sprawl and revive the inner cities. Part of the success in building more densely was to build smaller homes. The movement in the design and construction world for building the "not so big house" coincided with the "new urbanism" movement. With smaller homes came the awareness of the need to provide neighborhoods with a "3rd place."

The "3rd place" provides another "room" for you to experience a restoring or relaxing space, without it being in your home, therefore relieving you from the potential feeling of being "cramped" in your "not so big home."

A 3rd place provides opportunities for regular social engagement which fosters the building of relationships and community connectedness. The "3rd place" concept was portrayed in the 90s TV sitcom "Friends," starring Jennifer Aniston and Mathew Perry. In this show, the "Central Perk" coffee shop was the go-to neighborhood hang-out space the characters often frequented as their "3rd place."

The "3rd place" concept was also exemplified in the 80s TV sitcom "Cheers," starring Ted Danson and Shelley Long. The theme song for that show was "Where Everybody Knows Your Name."

The chorus line goes:
> *"Sometimes you want to go where everybody knows your name*
> *And they're always glad you came*
> *You wanna be where you can see*
> *Our troubles are all the same*
> *You wanna be where everybody knows your name."*

The reason that I bring up a "3rd place" as a consideration for your criteria in your selection of your post-retirement neighborhood is that having an easily accessible, even walkable, "3rd place" location near your home will add to your sense of belonging in a community, will get you out of your house, and will provide you a go-to place to meet with neighborhood friends on a regular basis, therefore strengthening your friendships and socialization. Frequency is key to developing relationships and becoming an integral part of a community. This "3rd place" most likely will be where you connect with 'your tribe.'

Have you ever put off inviting friends over to your home because you did not have the time or energy to clean your home to look presentable enough, to your standards, to entertain? Well, with a "3rd place," you gather with your friends at that place and forget about dealing with preparing your home for entertaining.

❈

Maybe easy access to a mass transit stop is something you want in your neighborhood because you see that as you get older that is the mode of transportation of choice for you. Remember, having readily available access to a mode of transportation, whether that is walking, biking, bus, etc., to draw you out of your house to connect to your community and keep you socially active, will be medicine to your soul. When you are in your 60s and 70s, and most of your 80s, you may not have any difficulty with driving. So, you may not think about needing certain places close enough to access without having to jump in a vehicle to get there. But as you continue to age, your priorities for your ideal neighborhood will change somewhat.

Both you and your friends may be unable to drive in your later years. With that said, you may decide that living in a sparsely populated rural area may make it too challenging to keep up with your social connections, which may be a priority to you.

Access to reliable mass transportation is something that could help support you living independently as you age, as it will allow you to continue going places that keep you socially and mentally engaged and thriving even when your physical ability prevents you from driving.

My grandmother, who lived independently in her home (with hired help to assist with cooking, housekeeping, managing a household, providing necessary transportation, and shopping) until she was 99 years old, had to give up her driver's license in her mid-90s when she could no longer drive safely. Her legs started getting weaker and it made it difficult to react quickly on the roads. Later in life she even had difficulty getting in and out of a car as a passenger, and her allergies prevented her from going outside much, so she became home bound.

She was a very social person and missed going to her church, walking in the mall, and visiting neighbors and friends. There was a time after my grandfather had passed, and after she had lost her ability to drive that she felt very alone and isolated because she was not engaging in regular social interactions, given her limited access. Her grown children had already passed away, and all but one grandchild lived out of state. So, she did not have regular visits from the family.

Eventually an elderly neighbor who did come to visit my grandmother on occasion introduced my grandmother to some of her card-playing friends, and eventually my grandmother started to have new friends come to visit her on a regular weekly basis. Friendships sustain life.

My grandmother passed away during the first year of the COVID-19 pandemic and I believe what weakened her already suppressed immune system was that her social circle had disbanded during COVID. Her friends would call, but they did not meet in person, and it was not the same...physical socializing has significant effects on the human spirit.

When researching neighborhoods, you may want to look into intentionally planned communities, such as retirement senior communities and co-housing communities. There are intentional communities for residents 55+ and there are also inter-generational communities.

Co-housing developments, a type of planned community, are designed to support intentional neighborly interaction, therefore strengthening the sense of community and belonging.

The concept of cohousing, which originated in Denmark in the 1960s, is an innovative approach to housing where private homes are clustered around inviting common spaces and communal facilities, in a walkable and socially engaging environment where the residents are actively involved in leading their community's operations, management, maintenance, and social activities. Regular planned activities, where residents share in the responsibilities of property operation and maintenance, a property design that promotes intentional neighbor interactions, and routine community gatherings like weekly meals together and community workdays, foster the building of a village-like community where it is expected of you to look out for the well-being of your neighbor.

The reason I highlight this type of community as ideal to support Aging-in-Place is that you will come to a time in your life where you are living alone, either as a widow or a single, when you are physically challenged and need the help of someone to assist you with a task you are working on but you aren't able to do it alone. This is when you wish you could call on a neighbor for a helping hand. This type of community has been developed on the value that neighbors help neighbors and you look out for one another. You become a tribe.

What if you were sick and have been home bound for over a week and no one called to see how you were doing? Wouldn't you wish you had someone who checked in on you to make sure you were doing okay or asked if they could get you something you needed from the store when you felt too sick to go yourself?

The co-housing development model was created to build a strong sense of community that fosters neighborly connections to be personable and close. In this type of community, a neighbor would know when anyone in their neighborhood was sick and would feel comfortable checking in on them. If you did not show up for the weekly community dinner or if you were home bound and weren't seen out in the courtyard or in the community garden, your neighbors would start to be concerned and inquire about you.

I would imagine that in the majority of the typical suburban neighborhoods across our country, a neighbor would feel somewhat uncomfortable asking another neighbor for help because community connections and neighborliness are not intentionally fostered. Regular neighbor interactions have decreased as we have become more technologically advanced and socially independent in our modern times.

Demographics, a strong sense of community connectedness, activities, facilities, and amenities are features you should consider in your priority list for selecting the neighborhood that will support you to Age-in-Place.

In your priority list, create a column beside each priority you have listed and note what aspects of that specific priority will support your goal to live independently longer and live well.

For example, if you chose to live in a neighborhood that was walkable to adequate mass transportation you would write that it will keep you from being car dependent, reduce your expenses for car maintenance, insurance, and fuel, and keep you socially and physically active even when you no longer can drive.

Or better yet, you may want to be in a neighborhood that has a high walkability score and is bike friendly, so you can putter around on your stable three-wheel bike to the grocery store, bank, salon, café, senior center, town park, to complete your errands all while getting your daily dose of outdoor exercise. Some towns in Switzerland are planned with a bike-heavy focus as a predominant means of transportation around town. Basel, Switzerland is on my list of places to visit in the near future.

You get the idea. Now create your vision and list your priorities for your ideal neighborhood.

PLANNING EXERCISE 1: CREATE A VISION BOARD

Describe with words and images what you **appreciate *in your* current *neighborhood*** and what additional features you **wish it had** to make it an ideal location to Age-in-Place. The following are images of the features I appreciate in my current neighborhood.

Images of My Ideal Neighborhood to Age-in-Place

These sample photos were photographed in Sonoma, CA by Rani Guram.

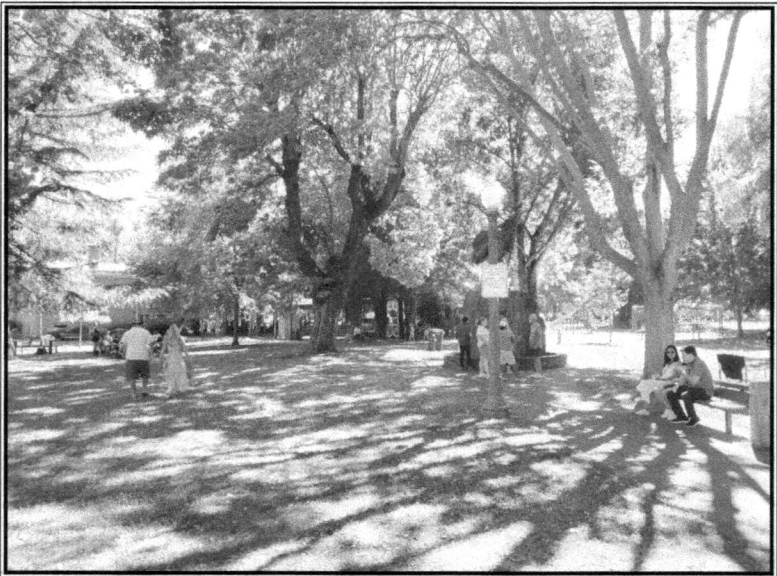

A centralized community park-like plaza
that regularly hosts community festivities

Weekly farmers' market with local organic produce and crafted foods

Serene walking paths to exercise and socialize

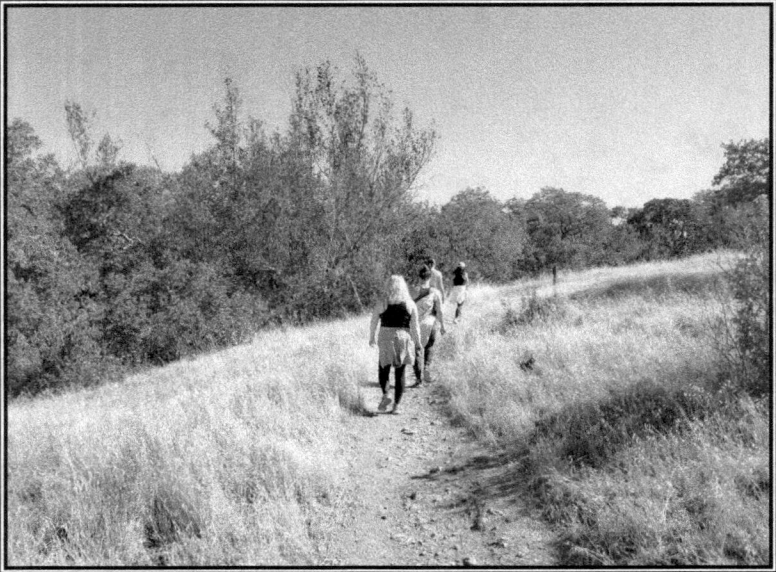
Outdoor recreation opportunities in a beautiful natural environment

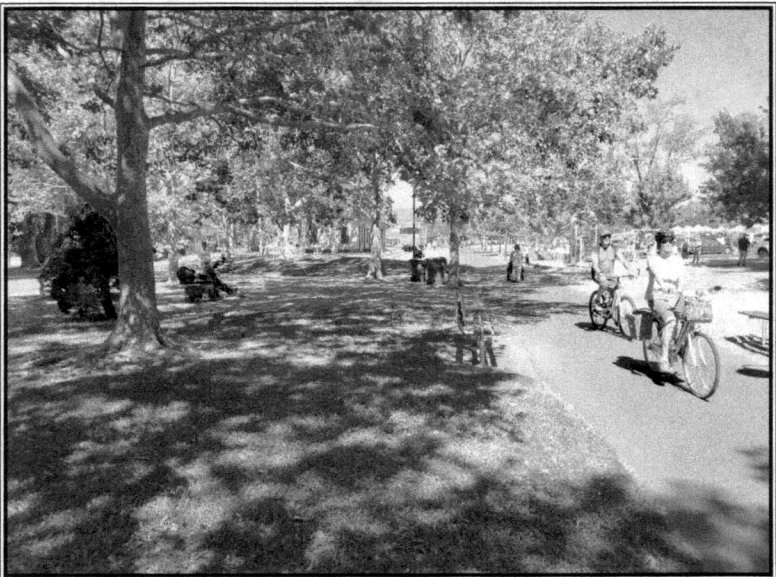
Safe and well-traveled bike paths to get about town

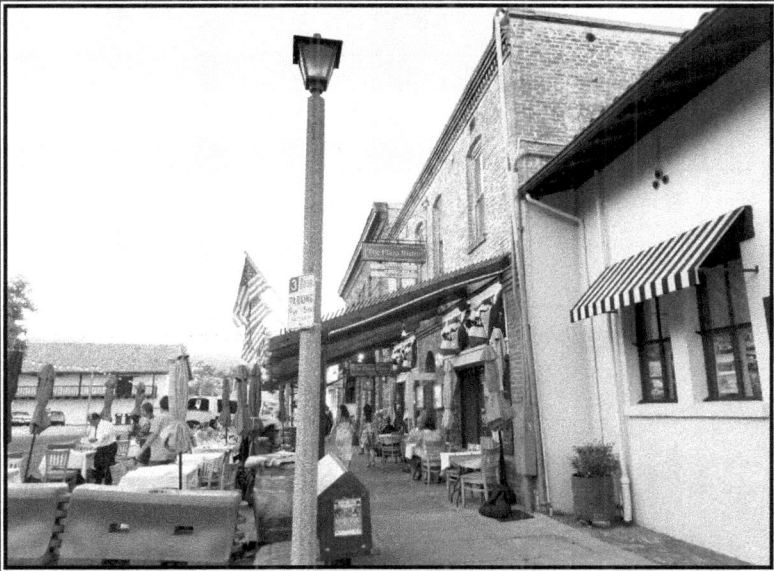

Easily accessible entertainment and 3rd place venues

PLANNING EXERCISE 2:
NEIGHBORHOOD PRIORITIES

Prioritize the top features you expressed in Exercise 1 and then specifically describe how each will support you to Age in Place.

1. Priority: _____

This priority will help me to Age-in-Place because:

_____

2. Priority: _____

This priority will help me to Age-in-Place because:

_____

3. Priority: _____

This priority will help me to Age-in-Place because:

_____

4. Priority: _____

This priority will help me to Age-in-Place because:

_____

5. Priority: _____

This priority will help me to Age-in-Place because:

_____

❖

CHAPTER 10

Choosing the Right Home
to Age-in-Place

"To us, our house was not insentient matter—it had a heart, and
a soul, and eyes to see us with; and approvals, and solicitudes,
and deep sympathies, it was of us, and we were in its confidence,
and lived in its grace and in the peace of its benediction."

MARK TWAIN, JANUARY,1897

These sample photos of Sonona were photographed by Rani Guram.

So far in this journey to plan to Age-in-Place, we have defined our ideal city and neighborhood, and have prioritized the features that make these personally ideal for us. Now let us discuss the characteristics for the type of home that would best support your aging needs and desired lifestyle as you progressively age from post-retirement to your twilight years so you can live well, independently longer, as you Age-in-Place.

As an architect, with a specialization in residential design, I understand how important the design of the home is to the level of comfort, efficiency, functionality, safety and sense of contentment a person will experience in their home environment. The design of your home can create a nurturing environment of solace, safety, security, stability, and comfort or it can contribute to your level of frustration, uncertainty, and anxiety.

Specific features of a home's design will support Age-in-Place goals. The features we will discuss in this chapter will help you create your personal priority list for the features you feel would most benefit you in living independently longer, in your own home, throughout your age progression.

When considering the important features to support aging-in-place in your home, consider the list you created in the chapter 4 exercise where you identified the personal challenges you need to plan for your Much Older You. The lack of mobility and flexibility in both mind and body and the rising costs to maintain, manage, and operate a home will be challenges we all face and must address.

In this chapter, we will discuss the features that can help us over-come these challenges. At the end of this chapter, you will have the opportunity to create a game plan that identifies and priori-tizes the features to look for and plan for in your ideal Age-in-Place home design.

Form

Let's start out with selecting the style or form of a home that will suit your Much Older You. A house on the ground level, with *no steps* is ideal. This type of home is often referred to as a ranch style home or a patio home. A home with the least number of steps is going to be the one that most supports someone who has restric-tions in mobility. You can find examples of a 'no step home' in a single-family home and a multi-family home.

What to do if you don't choose a 'no step home'? If there are one or two steps up to the front porch or landing, you can always add an aftermarket ramp. If you plan to stay in your existing home and it is a 2-story home, consider modifying your home to create a bathroom and bedroom on the ground level, if the floor plan is not laid out like that already. You can also add a chair lift between the floors.

Chair lift options can be an attachment to your stair run or a free-standing vertical transport. Chair lifts require less space and mechanisms than a traditional residential elevator. There are sev-eral types to choose from. Some chairlifts are standalone pieces of equipment with a partially enclosed platform that rises from one floor to the other, and other types of chairlifts are adaptations to the existing stair run that will move a wheelchair up and down the stairs.

With technology always advancing, keep your eyes open for new research and development in residential chair lifts and other items that support accessibility and mobility needs to assist the physically challenged to live independently.

Exterior

As for the exterior of the property, consider what level of care your Much Older You will want to or can put into maintaining a yard. As you become less flexible, it will become more difficult to continue doing your yard work and the cost will continue to rise to contract services such as landscaping, lawn mowing, and trimming bushes as well as the cost for irrigation. With that said, you may want to have a small yard with no lawn but rather xeriscaping, or consider living in a condominium complex where the Homeowners Association takes care of maintaining the landscaping and the upkeep of the building's exterior. Even if you only own a patio space or deck in your condo home, you still have the option to have some potted plants or raised plant beds if you have a green thumb and the need to get your hands in the soil.

For a second, I want you to think about the Much Older version of you, and try to imagine the amount of energy and resources it will take to maintain a yard and keep up the exterior of your home. If you keep things simple, you can still enjoy having a nice outdoor space but with less cost and hassle. There are lots of great landscaping design books out there on ways to have a beautiful landscape without the level of maintenance and water required by traditional landscape designs.

Another consideration regarding a home's exterior is the type of materials. Choose materials that require less maintenance and/or more affordable maintenance and that contribute to the home's efficiency. Choosing Hardi plank Siding and corrugated metal or 40-year asphalt shingle roofing materials that require low maintenance are some suggestions, but your geographical location influences the materials that will be most appropriate for that environment.

Consider the benefits of living in a newer home when you are older. You will reduce the headaches and inconveniences that come with managing home repairs.

Think *low maintenance* and *low operating costs* when choosing a home.

Size

Of course, a smaller home will be simpler to clean, manage, maintain, and operate, so consider buying or building only what is necessary and useful. There is no need to have extra rooms in your home that will require resources and energy to maintain and operate if you rarely use them. They could potentially end up as spaces to hoard 'stuff' in.

When you move to your Age-in-Place home, that is the ideal time to truly downsize, economize, and simplify your life. An organized space contributes to a more organized mind and lifestyle, therefore freeing up your mind, energy, time and resources to do more purposeful and essential activities in life that support your happiness, health, and well-being.

Remember, continuing to hold onto things that you do not regularly use will just require more space in your home to store these things. I recommend doing a purge as you prepare to transition into your Age-in-Place home. If your grown children have been storing things in your garage, it is time that you give them the ultimatum to either move their belongings to their own home or you will donate them. It's a 'tough love' move, but honestly everyone can benefit from taking a more minimalist approach to life. The fewer things you have in your home, the easier it will be to organize and find what you need, when you need it.

A cluttered home reflects and contributes to a cluttered mind, and vice versa. Keeping your home environment simplified and organized will contribute to your sense of composure and confidence, and it will keep more money in your purse. If you organize your home to easily locate things, it will save you time and money. With efficiency, you gain back life. As you age, reducing the need to recall your thoughts and retrace your steps will become more valuable to you. Did you ever need a tool for a task but did not remember where in your home or garage you placed it? So instead of digging around in the storage closet or searching in the garage for it, you decide to just go buy a new one? Well, if you keep your home, garage, office, closets, drawers, etc., organized in such a way that everything has a specific place to be stored and your things are organized in such a way to easily remember where something is placed, you will save money, energy, and time, and reduce frustration.

⌐◈⌐

If you are shopping for a new home, think smaller, more efficient, and accessible. I believe a two-bedroom/ two-bathroom home is ideal for a single or a couple to Age-in-Place. A two-bedroom home allows for the second bedroom to become your home office with a day bed for the occasional guest. Taking a long-term perspective, a guest bed—such as a Murphy Bed—may come in handy should you have the occasional guest or need occasional overnight assistance if you find you are not well enough or strong enough to be home by yourself due to an unexpected downturn in your health.

It's a good idea to have a room that is multipurpose so it can be used daily as an office, exercise room, or craft room that you regularly use, but can be converted to a sleeping room when needed by furnishing it with a futon, daybed, or Murphy Bed, etc. Consider that hospital visits may occur more often when you are older, when you are more susceptible to falling due to lack of balance and declining muscle strength. After a hospital stay, if you are not able to manage your daily living requirements, you might need to go to a skilled nursing facility for recovery and stay there until you can independently manage your daily living tasks before returning home. But if you have someone who is staying overnight with you and checking on you during the day, then you are more likely to be released earlier from the skilled nursing facility to go home.

The traditional single-family home is built as a 3 bedroom-2 bath home because they are designed for the average American family size. There are few single-family homes that are smaller than that and they usually were built earlier in the century. However, you can find newer 2 bedroom-2 bath homes as condominium units or town homes.

If you choose a 3 bedroom-2 bath single family house, keep it small so you have less to maintain, clean, and operate. A smaller, well insulated, low-maintenance home will save you time, frustration, and money, not only in the operational requirements and utilities, taxes, and insurance, but also in contracting services to maintain your home and yard when you no longer can do it yourself.

⤝✦⤞

An alternative approach to living in a larger than useful single-family home is to have roommates. You may be thinking the Much Older You will not have the patience to tolerate roommates. But remember the 80s sitcom TV show "The Golden Girls," starring Betty White as Rose Nylund?

In the TV show, three senior women along with one elderly mother all lived under one roof. One woman owned the house and rented the other three rooms to her friends. Sure, they had personality differences with the occasional interpersonal conflicts, but their friendship, camaraderie, and emotional support for one other outweighed the inconveniences and frustrations and became the anchor in sustaining a vibrant and contented quality of life throughout their senior years. Not only could one benefit from the emotional and social support of this type of sisterly arrangement, but it would also save quite a bit on housing expenses because the costs for property taxes, insurance, utilities, mortgage payment, and maintenance are shared by all roommates/residents instead of just the one who owned the house.

Don't limit your possibilities of finding the best Age-in-Place home environment for you because of your own limited imagination or preconception of inconveniences and obstacles. Where there is a will, there is a way.

Interior Space

Now let's turn our focus to the ideal space layout of the home, as spatial relationships between rooms and furnishings within the room will have a direct impact on the functionality of the home to how well it will support you to "Age-in-Place."

Consider the rooms that your Much Older self will tend to use the most as you become less mobile. These rooms most likely will be your bedroom, bathroom, and kitchen. Having these rooms easily accessible and in close proximity to one another is ideal. If you haven't spent much time with elderly parents for extended periods of time, you may not understand the challenges they face in circulating between these three rooms several times a day.

When my grandmother and dad were in their last few years of life, they took more naps during the day, and they made more trips to the bathroom. The third room was where they would spend most of their time sitting during their waking hours. For my grandmother, it was sitting at the kitchen table; for my dad, it was sitting in his office chair in front of the computer, which was his main mode of socializing and pastime.

Right now, you may not consider a route from your kitchen to your bathroom that is a distance of 30 to 40 feet a difficult feat, but it seems like miles when you are older and using a walker and your steps become smaller and more painful.

I recall when my grandmother was in her late 90s, the hallway which she had gone down so many times to reach her master bathroom had then become a challenge for her to get down in a timely manner. In her late 90s, there were many times my grandmother did not make it to the bathroom in time. Because wearing adult diapers were uncomfortable for her, she took the risk of having to change her clothes if she did not make it to the bathroom in time. And the process of changing her clothes would take her over

30-45 minutes because everything takes longer when your agility has diminished, and you are limited in bending and reaching.

～❖～

Consider now how you move in and around your house and consider how that may change in the future for your Much Older You as you progressively Age-in-Place.

Would it be easy to get from your garage to your back door to your kitchen to bring in and put away the groceries?

Do you have steps in your home that will later become a challenge? Even just one step can become a hurdle to someone who has weak leg muscles or lacks balance. Would you have enough room to maneuver safely in your bathroom if you had a walker or a wheelchair?

Consider how you get in and out of the shower or tub and dry off and change clothes. Would you be able to maneuver in your bathroom if you were not as stable or balanced?

Having a bathroom that is handicap accessible to accommodate your limitations as you become more physically challenged with age is key to having a successful Age-in-Place home. As we age, we tend to make more trips to the bathroom both day and night. There may come a time when you will need to place a portable toilet next to your bed because you are unable to transition quicky enough from your bed to your bathroom.

Planning ahead, you can create a more functional space so that your toilet in your master bathroom is easily accessible from your bed. The distance and effort to access the toilet from the bed needs to be simple, easy, and as safe possible. Many elderly fall in the bathroom, when transitioning on or off the commode, transitioning in and out of the tub or shower, and even while standing at the vanity to brush teeth or rinse the face. That is why bathrooms are so important to have remodeled or designed for safety and accessibility for an Age-in-Place home.

You can reference the Americans with Disability Act (ADA) Accessibility Guidelines for design information that will support creating spaces for Aging-in-Place. These design guidelines have been developed to create spaces that accommodate the physical limitations of the physically challenged. The guidelines take into consideration the location of grab bars, the height of the toilet, turning space for a wheelchair, reach distance, counter height, door widths, easy to use hardware, and many other parameters.

If you take a proactive approach, you will remodel your bathroom to meet your future physical limitations before you need it, because when the time comes that you actually need to use an accessible bathroom you most likely will not have the motivation nor the energy to endure the construction project.

Other ideas to consider in a bathroom remodel are installing a no-step shower with a bench, or a walk-in tub. Install features such as accessible height toilets (taller than the average toilet seat), or better yet a self-cleaning toilet, such as Toto toilet.

Technology Can Help

Automating tasks by utilizing self-cleaning fixtures or robotic appliances and accessories are technological approaches that can help free up your time, money, and energy so you can spend fewer resources on keeping up your home and more time on things you find enjoyable and meaningful. Automated fixtures and appliances are more costly up front, but in the long run they will save you time and energy.

There will come a time when you cannot manage to clean your toilet and tub, or vacuum your floor, or dust your shelves, or wash and fold clothes, cook your meals and wash your dishes. So either you pay someone to clean, or you push a button and let technology do it for you. I am excited to see new robotics being invented to help us manage our home life.

Visit our community website **Efficiency4Life.com** to read our latest posts about products that can make your life simpler and safer.

Though our society has become more isolated, in some ways, with technology promoting virtual social and business interactions instead of physical, I do believe technology will help us in our quest to live more efficiently, effectively, and more independently longer. New inventions to assist with hearing, seeing, and mobility; automated processes and robotics that increase efficiency; artificial intelligence, machine learning, innovative communication tools, "internet of things," and the evolving innovation of technology can help our seniors make their lifestyles and living environments more conducive to Aging-in-Place.

The goal is to create a home where you can live independently as long and as enjoyably as possible.

Efficiency and Functionality

When creating a space that supports Aging-in-Place, consider how the furnishings are arranged in a room to support accessibility and functionality. In a bedroom, the location of the furnishings that store your clothes, laundry, undergarments, and accessories is important to maneuvering efficiently around your room. There may come a day that you would greatly benefit from accessing all of these while sitting on your bed.

Take the time to study your personal movement routines and habits and see where you can make them more efficient through the placement and organization of your things, especially the items you use most often.

The strategy to make your dwelling Age-in-Place supportive is to be conscious of what things, actions, activities, and movements are causing frustration, challenges, and inefficiencies. Understand why. Then look for a solution to make your home more suitable for your aging needs.

Think of how to reduce the number of steps, twists, turns and bending you must do to maneuver around the room and home to perform your daily routines. Consider the effort it would take if you used a walker or were in a wheelchair and you needed to take clothes from a laundry hamper to the washer, then the dryer, and then take clothes out of the dryer, fold them, and place them into the dresser drawer or hang them in the closet.

Try to keep the rooms and essentials for necessary and regular activities easily accessible and in close proximity to one another, such as installing a washer and dryer near the master bedroom. Think about the convenience of having a toilet room, sometimes called a powder room, near a kitchen and near the garage so you don't have to travel down the hallway to make that last call to the bathroom before you head out the door. Having shoes and socks in an attractive container or cabinet drawer near the door to the garage may cut down on the movements you take to put on your shoes before you leave the house.

Think not only about the strategic adjacency of rooms but also the relationship of things within a room. A well thought out kitchen layout with strategic placement of utensils, cook ware, dishes, pantry items, and appliances can reduce your number of turns, twists, and bends and greatly improve your functional experience and efficiency in your kitchen.

⊰❖⊱

When you think about creating an Age-in-Place home, you need to picture how your home can be modified to support the Much Older You when your agility declines and physical limitations increase.

For example, can you widen the doorways to specific rooms you will frequent often such as your bedroom and bathroom to accommodate the width of a wheelchair or a walker? Some walkers do not easily pass through the narrower doors of older homes. Consider widening doorways to make a three-foot opening to easily accommodate the passage of a wheelchair or motorized scooter to the rooms you will use the most.

Some beneficial alterations/modifications to plan for are changing the height of your cabinets and shelving in your kitchen and bathroom for easier reach and use, change to an ADA handicap accessible toilet, install grab bars near toilets, and purchase an after-market prefabbed ramp to place over steps. Based on your personal limitations (physical, mental, visual, etc.) the ideal locations you choose for furnishings and items you utilize on a daily basis will be different.

Consider your reach...for example, how easily can you access your dishwasher, clothes washer, and the clothes in your closet? The reach requirements for a wheelchair-bound individual will be different than the reach requirements for an individual using a walker who is challenged with bending over and prefers to remain upright. Some solutions to accommodate limited reach are to utilize dishwashers that pull out like drawers in a base cabinet and clothes washer and dryer units that can be set on pedestals. New products are being designed and manufactured to accommodate accessibility and support efficiency and convenience.

Identify what you need in your space and where it should be located so you can maneuver and function/operate well in these rooms, especially your kitchen, bathroom, bedroom, and the room you tend to spend most of your daytime in.

✦

To recap this chapter...as you get older and your physical energy and agility decreases, it will become more challenging to accomplish home maintenance and routine home chores and even daily living tasks such as cooking, cleaning, and bathing, etc. With this in mind, try to economize and minimize the effort spent on these tasks by downsizing in home size and yard size and keeping your house strategically arranged and organized to increase functionality, efficiency, and safety. Keep your home simple to clean, easy to maintain, and economical to operate.

In this chapter we have discussed key features of a home and home design that support Aging-in-Place. Now complete the planning exercise to create your **personal priority list** of the features important to you so you know what to look for in a new home you are shopping for or use the list as a 'to do' list of the features you plan to modify in your existing home. This will give you a game plan for developing your Age-in-Place home.

If you plan to keep living in your existing home, and are creating a list of modifications to make your home Age-in-Place friendly, then next to each feature on your list assign a milestone date (such as 1 yr., 5 yr., 10 yr. after retirement) as to when you plan to make that specific modification. This will help you know what you need to budget for and when you should take action to make the modification.

It is easy to not want to do any modifications until the time comes when you need it. Unfortunately, at that time you most likely will not have the time, patience, nor energy to coordinate or endure the construction process.

Drafting your game plan now with milestone timelines for action, will give you peace of mind that you are taking appropriate action to support the Much Older You to live independently longer in your own home.

PLANNING EXERCISE:
CREATE YOUR AGE-IN-PLACE HOME

What are the features of my ideal Age-in-Place home that will best support my Much Older self to live independently longer? (Prioritize them 1 to 10, 1 being the highest priority.)

1.

2.

3.

4.

5.

6.

7.

8.

9.

10.

What are the three to four rooms my Much Older Me will frequent most and should be in close proximity to each other?

1.

2.

3.

4.

In each of the rooms listed above, how can I organize and arrange things or automate activities in each of these spaces to reduce the turns, twists, bends, and steps to increase functionality and to operate more efficiently and safely in?

1.

2.

3.

4.

What are my daily or weekly living routine activities that need to be more efficient or accessible to support my Much Older self (ex. washing clothes, preparing meals, administrative and record keeping tasks, cleaning the bathroom and kitchen)?

1.

2.

3.

4.

5.

If planning to stay in your existing home, what modifications do you plan to make and when do you plan to make them (1 year, 5 years, 10 years after retirement)?

Make a list of desired Age-in-Place modifications and assign a milestone date to each for when you plan to start that specific project.

PROJECTS FOR YEAR 1:

1.

2.

3.

4.

PROJECTS FOR YEARS 2-5:

1.

2.

3.

4.

PROJECTS FOR YEARS 6-10:

1.

2.

3.

4.

CHAPTER 11

You Have a Plan: Now Go Forth!

"Whether you think you can, or you
think you can't–you're right."

HENRY FORD

Considering our Much Older selves and how we will manage when our bodies and minds slow down, and the fact that we may be doing life alone, can be scary to think about, especially if we do not plan for it.

This book was written to help you plan for your appropriate post-retirement home environment that will support you to live independently, securely, and comfortably, in a familiar and supportive environment where you can enjoy the last decades of your life with less stress and less uncertainty. Coming up with an **'Age-in-Place' game plan** will give you peace of mind. It will help you take a deep look into the future, so you are prepared to face it in the best manner possible.

If you contemplate the information and complete the exercises in this book, and take action to implement what you have learned, you will be empowered to find the appropriate home environment (city, neighborhood, and home) that will support you to live independently longer through your twilight years. Use the personal priority lists you created in the previous chapters as your game plan to start preparing for your Age-in-Place home. Your personalized game plan will guide you to choose and create the supportive living environment that will be best suited for you. Connect often with the online community Efficiency 4 Life (Efficiency4Life.com) for the latest information and ideas that can support your goal to live independently longer.

The on-line community website Efficiency4Life.com provides a platform for readers to glean from others personal experiences, routines, practices and solutions for what has helped them to successfully 'Age-in-Place.' On the website, the community will share helpful information such as recommendations for towns that are conducive to Aging-in-Place, space planning and space organization ideas to make your daily living tasks easier to manage, suggestions of products and services that can support your independence and help you automate tasks when possible, and many other interesting and useful topics.

Part of Aging-in-Place successfully is to be a part of a like-minded and encouraging community where members can discuss issues that others in the group can relate to and where you can learn from one another, and together help each other to 'Age-in-Place.'

Efficiency 4 Life (Efficiency4Life.com) is your mastermind community that desires to live more efficiently and effectively in carrying out day-to-day activities and creating home environments that help gain back time, energy, and resources, so that we can live more connected, purposeful, and empowered lives that thrive, especially as we age.

All my best to you in your pursuit to live well and live independently longer!

Let's plan to Age-in-Place.

We can do this!

❖

About the Author

Rani Guram has worked as an architect for over 30 years and one thing she loves about the work is creating built environments that are positive experiential spaces; spaces that comfort, console, cele-brate, welcome, inspire and support. She draws upon this experience to help you discover your best Age-in Place home that will support you to live longer and live well in your own home as you enjoy your retirement life and age into your twilight years.

Help Spread the Word... Leave a Review!

Thank you reader and friend for making an investment in yourself to prepare for your future by choosing to purchase this book and thoughtfully participating in the exercises to create your personal game plan for where to retire to set your (much older) self up for success, and how to choose/create a home environment that best supports you to age-in-place well.

If you found some benefit in reading this, I would love to hear from you. Will you please take two quick minutes to post a review on Amazon. Your review will help this book reach more readers and build an on-line community to support people who want to Age-in-Place.

You can hop on Amazon and Goodreads to leave a review for

The
LONGEVITY HOME
Where to Retire to Set Your
(Much Older) Self Up for Success

Much appreciated!
Rani